To,

THE GATEKEEPER

Take your position at the Gates – Genesis 22:17

Proverbs 8:34

18/12/18

IHERINGIUS

ISBN 978-0-9575354-8-0

A CIP catalogue record for this book is available from the British Library.

Iheringius
An imprint of
Joensuu Media Ltd
145-157 St John Street
London
EC1V 4PW
England

www.iheringius.com

THE GATEKEEPER

Bringing a Revolution and Mind-Shift to
Your Personal Prayer Life
and Prayer Movements in the Nations

DAVID MUYIWA ADEOLA

FOREWORD BY DR GEORGE ANNADORAI

CONTENTS

It is not enough for the believer to begin to pray, nor to pray correctly; nor is it enough to continue for a time to pray. We must patiently, believingly continue in prayer until we obtain an answer. Further, we have not only to continue in prayer until the end, but we have also to believe that God does hear us and will answer our prayers. Most frequently we fail in not continuing in prayer until the blessing is obtained, and in not expecting the blessing.

George Muller

ACKNOWLEDGEMENTS

MY PRAISE and thanks go to the Almighty God who gave me the prompting and mandate to write this new re-loaded version of the earlier book *City Gates: Watching Over the City Gates*. I could never have done anything without the inspiration of the Holy Spirit all through the writing and editing of this book. Even when I read it again, I'm astonished at the level of God's inspired word that could only have come from the heart of the Father Himself. Thank you Lord for using me to be your instrument and a blessing to the body of Christ!

A most worthy thanks goes to my brother, friend and co-worker in the Kingdom, Marko Joensuu, who tirelessly helped in the editing of this book. Your honesty and prayers were invaluable.

My thanks also go to Dr. George Annadorai, who is an encourager all the way.

And special thanks go to my friend and wife Kunbi, who gave me a most amazing support through prayers and encouragement all through the process and often appreciated her critical eyes for details that helped in many ways all through the process of writing this book. Thank you my love! I didn't expect any less from you.

My joy would be that everyone that reads, or better still, studies this book, that your prayer life will never be the same again.

FOREWORD

EACH YEAR I enter and exit the world's most important city gate—Jerusalem. While secularists insist that what is happening in Jerusalem is a political battle between Jews and Arabs, we as believers know that it is really a prophetic war between God and Satan, vying for the ownership of the world's most important city—Jerusalem.

Unknown to many, Jerusalem's destiny is to be the City of the Great King (Psalm 48:1–2) and the throne of the Lord (Jeremiah 3:17). We as Bible-believing Christians know for a fact that the King of this Great City is Jesus. But Satan is not convinced, and he has been waging a war that will ultimately demonstrate who the real King is.

Jerusalem is a city gate. This I know, as I have been waging warfare at this gate since 1998, when I first received the revelation as to what Jerusalem was, is, and will be. And one of the most important gates in Jerusalem is the Eastern Gate. The prophet Ezekiel told us that at some point in the future the glory of the God of Israel will pass through the *"gate facing east"* (Ezekiel 43:1–5).

Figuratively speaking, the Eastern Gate is where I live. The devil knows this, and therefore he has positioned his best troops—demonic principalities and powers—at these gates in the East, and they are the guardians of the seven gates—Animism, Shintoism, Buddhism, Communism, Hinduism, Islam and Judaism. And Jesus has to pass through these gates before He can enter Jerusalem. The greatest spiritual war will be fought at the city gates!

I want to congratulate my friend, brother and a fellow soldier on the front line of spiritual battles for writing this book at a time when we need it the most. It is a battle training manual written by a field-tested soldier. He has honed his skills into strategies that will prove to be an answer to many of our prayers.

May I commend you not only to read this book, but to buy it in bulk, and send it to all your colleagues who are battling daily at the city gates! They will be grateful, and you will be glad.

Before you read this book, commit yourself to the Lord of Hosts, asking Him to surround you with His angelic warriors, as you come face to face with the dark powers lurking at the city gates.

Apostle George Annadorai
January 12, 2016

THE JOURNEY

THIS BOOK is an outcome of the revelations I received over a decade of annual pilgrimages to Israel.

When I was in Israel in January 2009 on one of those journeys, I met with Avi Mizrachi—my good friend and a Messianic Jew. Messianic Jews are Jewish followers of Jesus who observe many of the Jewish traditions. The first Christians were Messianic Jews, and we can see in Acts how they worshipped in the Temple, perceiving following Jesus to be the fulfilment of Jewish prophecies about the Jewish Messiah. They were only forced to leave the Jewish community due to persecution.

But even Paul, known as the apostle to the Gentiles, went to a Jewish synagogue first when he entered any city.

Many adherents of Messianic Judaism are ethnically Jewish and argue that the movement is a sect of Judaism. Many refer to themselves in Hebrew as *maaminim* (believers), not converts, and *yehudim* (Jews), not *notzrim* (Christians). But Jewish organisations and the Supreme Court of Israel, in cases related to the Law of Return, have rejected this claim, and instead consider Messianic Judaism to be a form of Christianity.

Back to my story—Avi highlighted an important point, while telling us about the Jewish history and how the first modern Jewish immigrants came back to Israel through the Port (Gate) of Israel, located at Joppa in Tel Aviv.

Most Christian tourists that come to Israel land at Ben Gurion Airport near Tel Aviv and immediately board a bus to Jerusalem, and they are more than happy not to visit Tel Aviv, which they see more as a liberal beach party town not corresponding to their view of the

Holy Land, and certainly with no historical significance. But in fact, Tel Aviv has huge historical significance, especially when it comes to the birth of the modern Israel. The first modern immigration back to Israel began in 1882 and lasted until 1903, with around 25,000-30,000 Jews landing in the Promised Land. The immigration continued, and, eventually, on May 14, 1948, the State of Israel declared independence, as had been prophesied in Isaiah 66:8:

> Who has heard such a thing? Who has seen such things? Shall a land be born in one day? Shall a nation be brought forth in one moment? For as soon as Zion was in labor she brought forth her children.

The new nation had been birthed out of the Holocaust, as the world still felt guilty about letting over six million Jews be slaughtered, and looked favourably at the birth of the new nation.

The birth of the modern Israel was followed in 1950 by the Law of Return, which grants every Jew an automatic right to immigrate to Israel and become a citizen. With the gates wide open after statehood had been declared, a wave of mass immigration soon brought 687,000 Jews to Israel's shores, as they looked for refuge. They arrived through the ancient port city Jaffa—the biblical Joppa—which merged with Tel Aviv in 1950, as it was the main port.

This left a very strong impression on me, and I pondered about it long after I had come back from Israel. It was such a wonderful story, but this gateway to Israel had been ignored and forgotten by most pilgrims. I began to pray along the lines of Psalm 24, and as I did, God gave me more understanding.

Psalms 24:7-9 says,

> Lift up your heads, you gates; be lifted up, you ancient doors, that the King of glory may come in. Who is this King of glory? The Lord strong and mighty, the Lord mighty in battle. Lift up your heads, you gates; lift them up, you ancient doors, that the King of glory may come in.

Psalm 24 was composed by David, probably at the time of bringing the Ark of the Covenant to Jerusalem. When the Ark came to the

city, so came the presence of God, and it symbolised
rule of God over Jerusalem.

As I prayed this psalm over a season, I sensed that t.
to give me an understanding about what it means to enter the g...
when it comes to spiritual dimension. I also began to grasp that,
right now, we were unable to bring the light of Jesus to our cities
and transform them for the simple reason that the gates to our
cities were in the possession of our enemies. When it comes to the
power in our nation—in politics, business, legislation and so on—it
is largely not in the hands of righteous men and women. This leads
to an unrighteous rule and unrighteous society. We can see how
nearly everywhere in our society Christianity and Christian ethics
are losing ground. We might be winning some individual fights,
but we are losing the war.

I began to understand that God wanted us to take control of the gates in our cities—the places and channels of influence—so that we could be the gatekeepers in the spiritual and also the visible dimension, influencing and guarding our nations through prayer and action.

In Genesis 22:17 God promises Abraham,

Gates are not only physical, but they also have a spiritual dimension. The structures of power that we can see visibly always reflect spiritual realities.

> "I will surely bless you, and I will surely multiply your offspring as the stars of heaven and as the sand that is on the seashore. And your offspring shall possess the gate of his enemies."

We are the children of Abraham—the children of faith—and I
began to understand that this is not just a promise to the Jews, but
also a promise to us. What we can glean from this verse is that God
recognises that we will have enemies, but He promises that we can
possess the gates of our enemies—a life in victory!

Gates are not only physical, but they also have a spiritual
dimension. The structures of power that we can see visibly always
reflect spiritual realities.

When a parliament votes, for example, to approve same-sex marriage, there has been a spiritual shift that has enabled it to happen.

But to have spiritual authority to become gatekeepers of our cities, we need access to the power of Heaven. Figuratively speaking, we need to access the gates of Heaven.

When Jesus died on the cross, the veil that separated the Holy of Holies from the rest of the Temple and the world was torn.

Matthew 27:51 says,

> And behold, the curtain of the temple was torn in two, from top to bottom. And the earth shook, and the rocks were split.

This means that the separation between God and man has been removed. The gates of heaven have been opened to us, and that is why we can pray, *"Your kingdom come, Your will be done, on earth as it is in heaven."*

Psalm 100 says,

> Make a joyful shout to the Lord, all you lands!
> Serve the Lord with gladness;
> Come before His presence with singing.
> Know that the Lord, He is God;
> It is He who has made us, and not we ourselves;
> We are His people and the sheep of His pasture.
> Enter into His gates with thanksgiving,
> And into His courts with praise.
> Be thankful to Him, and bless His name.
> For the Lord is good;
> His mercy is everlasting,
> And His truth endures to all generations.

Because of Jesus we can now enter His gates with thanksgiving. And it is because this gate into the presence of God has been opened that we can have the spiritual authority to take possession of any other gates.

On September 2009, my next trip to Israel, after I had spoken with Avi Mizrachi, as we landed in Tel Aviv with our team of worshippers and intercessors, we went straight to Jaffa, so that we would enter Israel through the 'correct' gate, the gate that had given birth to the modern Israel. It is also the same port through which workmen of the King of Tyre brought the cedars of Lebanon in floats for transportation to Jerusalem, so that King Solomon could build the Temple.

While on the flight, the Holy Spirit had highlighted to me the Beautiful Gate. This Temple gate is mentioned in Acts 3—a lame man was laid there. He received his healing at this gate through the hands of Peter.

This was the first healing miracle of the Early Church, after the disciples had been filled with the Holy Spirit in Acts 2 and around 3,000 men had been saved after Peter's preaching. To do the work of being effective witnesses for Jesus, there has to be a demonstration of the power of the Spirit. The healing of the lame man at the Beautiful Gate was a sign of what was to come, and what Paul described in 1 Corinthians 2:4.

> And my speech and my message were not in plausible words of wisdom, but in demonstration of the Spirit and of power.

These two events—the conversion of the 3,000 and the healing of the lame man—demonstrate the Kingdom lifestyle that Jesus offers to His disciples even today.

Back to our trip. There was a great excitement in our team, as our hosts explained to us that the Hebrew name of the city—*Yafo*—actually means "beautiful". The Holy Spirit had been highlighting the Beautiful Gate to me, and I had shared that with my team, and now we were in fact entering the Beautiful Gate—in Jaffa, or in Tel Aviv!

In Tel Aviv, we went through the Ancient Gates of Israel in worship and intercession, declaring Psalm 24 together with the Messianic Adonai Roi congregation that have taken the role to be the gatekeepers. There was a sense of great breakthrough, and the presence of God brought confirmation that He had been speaking to us. We prayed with the team, as they took their position at the gates of their city. This congregation has recently opened a 24/7 Prayer House, and they are standing faithfully at this gate.

Chapter 1

THE PROMISE

"I will surely bless you, and I will surely multiply your offspring as the stars of heaven and as the sand that is on the seashore. And your offspring shall possess the gate of his enemies." (Genesis 22:17)

ABRAHAM IS THE FATHER OF FAITH, and the promise of Abraham belongs to us today. The aim of this book is to help the intercessors and believers to understand their authority when it comes to possessing the gates of their enemies. Those gates belong to us!

The same promise is repeated again as a prayer for Rebekah, as she leaves her family to marry Abraham's son Isaac in Genesis 24:60.

> And they blessed Rebekah and said to her, "Our sister, may you become thousands of ten thousands, and may your offspring possess the gate of those who hate them!"

This shows how the blessing and authority can pass from generation to generation. In the West, we have seen many great revivals and Christian movements that have transformed society, but today, we need another generation willing to step into the spiritual authority that God has purposed for the gatekeepers.

This book gives practical guidance on how to possess the gates of our enemies, and how to maintain control over the gates, once you walk in the spiritual authority needed to possess the gates.

The call of being a gatekeeper comes with great responsibility, as we must be able to take a stand in intercession for our city or nation. It is about partnering with the Holy Spirit and becoming a defender and custodian of God's purposes.

One of the simple, biblical ways of doing this is by interceding for all the MPs in Parliament, or representatives in the Congress, and other leaders, as Paul instructs in 1 Timothy 2:1-3:

> First of all, then, I urge that supplications, prayers, intercessions, and thanksgivings be made for all people, for kings and all who are in high positions, that we may lead a peaceful and quiet life, godly and dignified in every way. This is good, and it is pleasing in the sight of God our Savior.

This requires consistency, discipline and insight, as to pray effectively, you need to keep your eyes open on what is going on in your nation. It is not a lifestyle of isolation but involvement in society.

But above all, it is a lifestyle of prayer and worship. The gatekeepers during the time of King David were Levites and their focus was on worship and total commitment to God.

1 Chronicles 9:26-27 informs,

> For the four chief gatekeepers, who were Levites, were entrusted to be over the chambers and the treasures of the house of God. And they lodged around the house of God, for on them lay the duty of watching, and they had charge of opening it every morning.

It is vital to understand that being a gatekeeper was and is a *priestly* function. And gatekeeping started early in the morning, every morning, without fail.

Are you willing to take a stand for your nation? Do you consider yourself qualified? Then you must be ready for regular, persistent prayer for your nation.

I invite you to come on this journey with me and discover the thrill of being a gatekeeper!

Chapter 2

TAKING POSSESSION

"I will surely bless you, and I will surely multiply your offspring as the stars of heaven and as the sand that is on the seashore. And your offspring shall possess the gate of his enemies, and in your offspring shall all the nations of the earth be blessed, because you have obeyed my voice." (Genesis 22:17-18)

ALTHOUGH these verses contain a great promise of blessing, they also tell that the gates are in the hands of the enemies. God gives this promise to Abraham, who is a nomad, and he would have passed many walled cities, some of them friendly, many not. God promises that one day Abraham's offspring would own all that land! But to do that, they would have to take over the walled cities, as the land was controlled by them.

There is a great spiritual principle here, and it is applicable to us. This is God's promise to us also; we can see it in the Lord's Prayer, where we ask for God's Kingdom to come to earth. Whatever that means—and there are many possible interpretations—it must also mean that God's Kingdom will be manifested in our cities.

But our enemies have enjoyed their power at the city gates for a long time, and, therefore, they will not just leave their position. Hence, we have to be persistent in our prayer and intercession.

The spiritual principle here is that we will be able to take possession of those gates that God has promised to us. Like with Abraham, those gates are specific to our callings.

Deuteronomy 32:8 says,

When the Most High gave to the nations their inheritance, when he divided mankind, he fixed the borders of the peoples according to the number of the sons of God.

This is a verse that has troubled many Bible translators, and some have translated *"the sons of God"* either as 'the people of Israel' or as 'angels'. But Romans 8:14 says,

For all who are led by the Spirit of God are sons of God.

We are the sons of God through adoption; this means that we all have a land to possess—perhaps not a geographical land, but a spiritual land. Unfortunately, many Christians have passed on without ever reaching their God-given destiny. Often, they hadn't even started looking when they died! Indeed, it is possible to go through life without ever achieving what God has called you to, and I am sure, people can find many excuses for it.

But that is not the way of the gatekeepers.

What are the gates?

You might wonder why I have chosen to use the metaphor of gates to argue for the need of Christian influence—both spiritual and physically manifested—in our nation and cities. The answer is simple. It is a biblical metaphor for it, and although we are less dependent on physical gates in our cities than before, the metaphor is still fitting.

To me, gates are the passageways for 'entry and exit' in our society, manned by gatekeepers, which can be human beings or spiritual powers.

Some of the gates are physical, others invisible, but they all have a spiritual dimension.

They are the places of power, communication and transition in our society, and whoever controls them has a power over people's destiny. They can be personal, local, or national. For example, a blocked 'gate' in your workplace can obstruct your promotion, and the reasons behind that can often be spiritual.

Some of our national gates are the parliamentary system, our courts, airports, naval ports, train stations, social services and media. There are many others, and as a gatekeeper you will be able to identify the gates around you with more precision. These are the places where important decisions for our lives are made, and from where the whole society is influenced through media and communication tools.

Most of the gates in our society are in the hands of the enemies, and, consequently, the enemies of the gospel decide what goes in and what goes out. For example, the media, business and the politicians largely decide what conversations are 'correct' in our society, and they decide the nature of these conversations. Because of that, talking about Jesus in any challenging way has largely been banned in many parts of our society. And we see many decisions going against Christians in society—in courts, the police, social services, media, Parliament and so on.

The human gatekeepers are the decision makers in their areas, and they can be influenced by many forces—godly or ungodly, visible and invisible. It makes a big difference what those influences are. Often, we are deceived by an illusion of democracy when, in fact, decisions are made by a few gatekeepers. For example, the European Union has an aura of democracy when, in reality, it is mostly governed by unelected bureaucrats, whose decisions are influenced by lobby groups that most of us have never even heard of.

And behind the gates, an invisible, spiritual battle between God and the devil rages.

So, these gates are not all necessarily physical, but they can be also entirely spiritual. For instance, the gates of Heaven are not in any way physical, but spiritual.

Though it is not necessary to maintain a physical presence in order to be a gatekeeper at a physical gate, it might be necessary from time to time actually to visit that gate, as led by the Spirit of God, to make proclamations and declarations of whatever the Lord might be laying on our spirit.

This is what I would refer to as a *prophetic act*. I go to the gates of Parliament and the gates of 10 Downing Street, which is the residence and the office of the Prime Minister of the United Kingdom, to make proclamations.

Gates can be an entrance to a city, town or village. When you approach a city on the motorway, and you see a sign showing the name of that city, you are traveling on a gateway. The gateway might not have a physical gate, though some do. When I'm driving from New York to Canada, there is a checkpoint where the immigration officers check passports and ensure visitors have an entry visa. They are gatekeepers. These gates are manned at all times. Our airports are gateways, and they also need to be manned at all times. This is a spiritual principle applicable to us as gatekeepers.

Marketplace gatekeepers

God has not called us to serve mammon; He wants mammon to serve the Kingdom. There can be only one master, and if Jesus is our Master, then money must be our servant. But the work of the Kingdom is being stifled for lack of finances that are in the wrong hands at the gates—hands that are not serving God but mammon.

But because the whole earth is God's possession and handiwork, it stands to reason that God wants to raise up gatekeepers in the marketplace to be people of influence. These gatekeepers will see God as Master and money as the servant. This is only possible if we begin to recognise that our mandate extends beyond our church buildings. And if you are already positioned in the marketplace, you need to understand why you are there. You aren't just making a career for yourself in business, banking, the legal system and so on, but you are a representative of God's Kingdom.

1 Chronicles 9:26-27 says,

> For the four chief gatekeepers, who were Levites, were entrusted to be over the chambers and the treasures of the house of God. And they lodged around the house of God, for on them lay the duty of watching, and they had charge of opening it every morning.

Then verse 33 adds,

> Now these, the singers, the heads of fathers' houses of the Levites, were in the chambers of the temple free from other service, for they were on duty day and night.

These gatekeepers during King David's reign were 212 in number and appointed by King David and the prophet Samuel to guard the

Tabernacle. These gatekeepers were priests. Just before his death, David appointed 4,000 gatekeepers to offer praises to the Lord.

> "4,000 gatekeepers, and 4,000 shall offer praises to the Lord with the instruments that I have made for praise." (1 Chronicles 23:5)

From King Solomon's time, the Levites, who were the gatekeepers of the Temple, had charge over the treasuries of the house of God. We can see how in the Temple mammon was subject to God. It served God. These Levites had a very specific call, and God had separated them for that purpose. In a similar vein, God has called and anointed some to operate in the marketplace to be stewards of God's resources for the end-time harvest. Like in the Temple, today God wants to subject mammon through His servants, so that it will achieve His purposes.

The mandate of Matthew 28:18-20 to go and make disciples of all the nations goes way beyond just evangelism.

> And Jesus came and said to them, "All authority in heaven and on earth has been given to me. Go therefore and make disciples of all nations, baptizing them in the name of the Father and of the Son and of the Holy Spirit, teaching them to observe all that I have commanded you. And behold, I am with you always, to the end of the age."

What happens when people working in the government, Parliament, education or business become disciples? They begin to operate in those spheres following the principles and the values of God's Kingdom.

This is what happened with the Early Church. Initially, they were persecuted, but eventually Christians were in control of the government, commerce and even the military of the Roman Empire. It was only later when the Church lost her way. This is always the case with God's blessing and favour. Unless we keep on serving Him first, a blessing can easily become a curse.

We can see this in Deuteronomy 31:12-13 (NKJV), where Moses instructs the priests:

"Gather the people together, men and women and little ones, and the stranger who is within your gates, that they may hear and that they may learn to fear the Lord your God and carefully observe all the words of this law, and that their children, who have not known it, may hear and learn to fear the Lord your God as long as you live in the land which you cross the Jordan to possess."

Now, the Israelites were about to enter the Promised Land; it was a blessing, but we know from the history of Israel that taking possession of the gates is just the first part, and that once you have taken possession of them, it is so easy to forget that it was God who has given you the gates in the first place.

We need to take possession of the gates, because we are yet to finish with our commission of taking the gospel to all the nations.

In Matthew 24:14 Jesus says,

And this gospel of the kingdom will be proclaimed throughout the whole world as a testimony to all nations, and then the end will come.

Today, the gates to some of these nations are firmly shut, and it takes financing to reach out to their people. For example, in the Middle East the gospel has been preached effectively in the last few years through the internet and satellite TV, but doing that takes a lot of finance.

Taking possession of the gates is not *dominion* theology—a theocratic ideology that seeks to implement a nation governed by Christians ruling over the rest of society. It is walking in the promises of God.

How

We need to develop an awareness and discernment of where we are presently and understand how the enemy possesses our gates.

Also, we need to walk in obedience. This is not sin-free perfection but the obedience of Abraham, which means trusting in what God has promised to us and taking practical action on the basis of His promises.

A key area today is the marketplace, and we must begin to gather the Christians who have been called and commissioned by God to operate in the marketplace.

Church has largely ignored this area, and, consequently, many Christians working in the marketplace don't see their work as a calling and as part of the expansion of the Kingdom. A religious mindset separates the sacred from the secular, but in God's eyes all our life can and should be a service to Him.

Psalm 24:1 says,

> The earth is the Lord's and the fullness thereof, the world and those who dwell therein.

Both the Church and the world belong to God, but it doesn't mean that they always operate in God's will.

The marketplace gatekeepers are intercessors and watchmen, so if you want to become a marketplace gatekeeper, you must begin to pray.

It is not enough to operate in the marketplace, it is only enough to operate in the marketplace with the Lord.

We need teachers and mentors who understand what the gates are in the marketplace, and how to take possession of them. A preacher might be able to give you a good sermon, but it takes someone who is a disciple of Jesus and who operates as a professional in the marketplace to mentor other people in the same field.

It takes intentional action to lay hold of the gates of our city and nation. For example, William Wilberforce, whom God used in the area of politics to abolish slavery in Britain, toiled tirelessly for decades before he reached his goal.

John Wesley, the founder of Methodism, wrote a letter to William Wilberforce six days before he died. He said,

> Unless the divine power has raised you up to be as "Athanasius against the world," I see not how you can go through your glorious enterprise in opposing that execrable villainy, which is the scandal of religion, of England, and of human nature. Unless God has raised

you up for this very thing, you will be worn out by the opposition of men and devils. But if God be for you, who can be against you? Are all of them stronger than God? O be not weary of well-doing! Go on, in the name of God and in the power of His might, till even American slavery (the vilest that ever saw the sun) shall vanish away before it.

It took a man and a movement with the call from God, mentors such as John Wesley, relentless prayer and a long career in politics to bring slavery to an end. Let us be encouraged by men such as Wilberforce, who took possession of the gates of enemy in Parliament and forced change!

If you have been called to marketplace ministry, you must keep the words of Jesus in Matthew 6:24 close to heart.

No one can serve two masters, for either he will hate the one and love the other, or he will be devoted to the one and despise the other. You cannot serve God and money.

Watchmen and gatekeepers working together
2 Samuel 18:24-26 (NKJV) says,

Now David was sitting between the two gates. And the watchman went up to the roof over the gate, to the wall, lifted his eyes and looked, and there was a man, running alone. Then the watchman cried out and told the king. And the king said, "If he is alone, there is news in his mouth." And he came rapidly and drew near. Then the watchman saw another man running, and the watchman called to the gatekeeper and said, "There is another man, running alone!" And the king said, "He also brings news."

The scripture here clearly indicates that watchman and gatekeeper work together, in *unity*, but they have two distinct roles. While the watchman was on the lookout, the gatekeeper was stationed at his post in what seems like a fixed position. The watchman had a vantage point on the rooftop, where he could see everyone that was coming in or going out. He also moved around and raised an alarm to the king and others about what could be a potential danger to the city.

As watchmen, we must learn how to lift our eyes to Heaven to look and see what others cannot see. Watchmen are God's agents who watch, have an advance notice of things that are happening in the spiritual dimension and tell people about what is going on. Often, they are prophets.

They intercede, but gatekeepers usually have the responsibility to take action. This is where the gatekeeper responds, this response being dependent on the message that the watchman brings.

King David was also operating in the spiritual dimension. He was not left out of the whole scenario, as he was the one that actually discerned the kind of messenger that was approaching!

The king said, "*If he is alone, there is news in his mouth.*"

According to Revelation 5:10, we are kings and priests unto our God, so this is still relevant to us. But often, today, the kingly role is an *apostolic* role, as it requires a high level of spiritual authority.

This tells me one very important point that we have often failed to employ as the Church.

And this is *unity*.

We see in these verses how there were three levels of operation before the gate was ever opened—a watchman, king and gatekeeper.

Quite often, watchmen want to be lone rangers, as if they were the only ones that hear God, whilst the king also wants to act alone and, can, if acting without discernment, order the gatekeeper to open the door to the enemy.

But at all three levels people are able to hear God and will be more effective through affirming one another. The problem starts when each one wants to act alone or independently. They each have their roles in the Church but must always come together for the good of all.

For all that, the gatekeeper ultimately determines who goes in and out of the gate.

You will notice that neither the king nor the watchman instructed the gatekeeper to open the gates. They simply passed on the information one to the other: the watchman raised the alarm and gave advance notice, the king used his discernment to identify the personality of those approaching, while the gatekeeper, 1 believe, had to process this information and determine whether the gate should be opened or not. I believe he could either go back to the watchman or the king to reconfirm, if he had any doubt at all.

The king sat at the gates but was not the gatekeeper.

2 Samuel 19:8 says,

> Then the king arose and took his seat in the gate. And the people were all told, "Behold, the king is sitting in the gate." And all the people came before the king.

Nevertheless, the king rules, makes decrees and judges at the gates. Whatever pronouncements he makes at the gates are binding. That is why the role is often apostolic.

In our case, unlike King David who was imperfect, our King is Jesus, and He is the gate.

Whilst a gatekeeper can also function in the office of the watchman, the two roles are clearly defined in Scripture.

- Kings make decrees—Revelation 5:10, 1:6.
- Watchmen keep watch at the highest point—Ezekiel 3:17, 33:6-7.
- Gatekeepers open and close the door, and they also watch—John 10:3, 1 Chronicles 9:27, 33.

Chapter 3

REDEEMED BY THE BLOOD

IT IS FAITH in what Jesus accomplished on the cross and the promises of God that gives us the confidence to believe that we can have the spiritual authority needed to take possession of the gates. We don't stand in our own righteousness, but in the righteousness of *Yeshua HaMashiach* (Jesus in Hebrew)!

There are foreshadows of our great Redeemer in the Old Testament, and they show how, in a lesser way, our life follows the same spiritual principles that were demonstrated in the life of Jesus.

In Colossians 1:24, Paul writes,

> Now I rejoice in my sufferings for you, and I am completing in my flesh what is lacking in Christ's afflictions for His body, that is, the church.

Although it is only the blood of Jesus that could buy redemption, Paul still felt that his suffering somehow added to Christ's afflictions.

Abraham sacrificing Isaac

The story of Abraham sacrificing Isaac in Genesis 22:2 is familiar to most Christians. It foreshadows the Father sacrificing the Son on the cross. The Lord commanded Abraham to sacrifice his only son Isaac. Although Abraham had another son, Ishmael, before Isaac was born, God referred to Isaac as Abraham's *only* son, because he was the only promised son.

Ishmael was the result of Sarah and Abraham's impatience and their wavering faith. Isaac was the result of a miracle. He was the son God gave to Sarah, even when she was barren.

As they were nearing the place of the sacrifice, one could not possibly imagine what would have been going on in the mind of the young lad:

> And Isaac said to his father Abraham, "My father!" And he said, "Here am I, my son." He said, "Behold, the fire and the wood, but where is the lamb for a burnt offering?" (Genesis 22:7)

If you were in Isaac's position, you'd probably ask the same question, wouldn't you? And I'm not sure if the father's answer brought any comfort to Isaac in any way.

> And Abraham said, "My son, God will provide for Himself the lamb for a burnt offering." (Genesis 22:8)

This is the level of faith and trust in the Lord that is required for us to be effective gatekeepers: a resolute trust that God is fully able to do what He has promised. If He has told Abraham that in his seed the nations of the earth will be blessed, then He will do it, and Abraham was able to rest in this assurance of the fact that God is able to keep His word, even by resurrecting Isaac if necessary.

One thing that resonates with me is Isaac's reaction of not questioning Abraham any further. I'm sure many of us, especially in the West, would probably find an argument as to why we think Abraham had gone nuts, or think it's about time to do a runner, before the man commits murder! The boy had the quiet reassurance of a son who trusts his father and knows his father loves him. It is the childlike trust we had when we were young and our father would ask us to jump down, assuring us that he would catch us, and the confidence that he was able to do so, causing us to jump without giving it a thought. You had no iota of doubt that your father was able to catch you.

Abraham was assured and believed that the Lord was able to provide the lamb or bring Isaac back to life.

He went ahead with the offering, as soon as they got to Mount Moriah. There he built an altar, put the wood together, tied Isaac and placed him on the altar, ready to sacrifice him unto God. But as soon as he raised the knife, he heard the call of the angel.

And Abraham stretched out his hand and took the knife to slay his son. But the Angel of the Lord called to him from heaven and said, "Abraham, Abraham!" So he said, "Here I am." And He said, "Do not lay your hand on the lad, or do anything to him; for now I know that you fear God, since you have not withheld your son, your only son, from Me." (Genesis 22:10-12, NKJV)

Abraham did not withhold his best from God, his only son, child of the promise. We must be able to let go of what we consider to be our best, knowing that our Father provided it in the first place, and trust that He is able to provide an alternative.

And Abraham lifted up his eyes and looked, and behold, behind him was a ram, caught in a thicket by his horns. And Abraham went and took the ram and offered it up as a burnt offering instead of his son. (Genesis 22:13)

Moriah means *the Lord will provide*!

And thank God, Abraham heard and recognised the voice of the Lord; otherwise the story would have ended differently. Another lesson for gatekeepers is how important it is to recognise the voice of the Lord!

However there was a substitute—a lamb, which represents the Lamb of God—that was slain for us, to take away the sins of the world.

Redemption at the gate

During the time of the judges when there was a famine, an Israelite family from Bethlehem—Elimelech, his wife Naomi, and their sons Mahlon and Chilion—emigrated to the nearby country of Moab. Elimelech died, and the sons married two Moabite women: Mahlon married Ruth and Chilion married Orpah. After about ten years, the two sons of Naomi also died in Moab. Naomi decided to return to Bethlehem. She told her daughters-in-law to return to their own mothers, and remarry. Orpah reluctantly left; however, Ruth said that she would rather follow Naomi back to Israel.

Ruth said to Naomi:

> "Entreat me not to leave you, or to turn back from following after you; for wherever you go, I will go; and wherever you lodge, I will lodge; your people shall be my people, and your God, my God." (Ruth 1:16)

Ruth and her mother-in-law arrived back in Bethlehem, where they met Boaz, a relative of Naomi's husband, who later became *kinsman-redeemer* to Ruth.

Ruth found favour with Boaz and was allowed to glean in his field.

> And at mealtime Boaz said to her, "Come here and eat some bread and dip your morsel in the wine." So she sat beside the reapers, and he passed to her roasted grain. And she ate until she was satisfied, and she had some left over. When she rose to glean, Boaz instructed his young men, saying, "Let her glean even among the sheaves, and do not reproach her. And also pull out some from the bundles for her and leave it for her to glean, and do not rebuke her." (Ruth 2:14-16)

Naomi and Ruth had come back to the town at the beginning of harvest.

> So Naomi returned, and Ruth the Moabite her daughter-in-law with her, who returned from the country of Moab. And they came to Bethlehem at the beginning of barley harvest. (Ruth 1:22)

They had come back empty-handed from Moab at the time of harvest, which was the best possible time to return. Arriving at the time of harvest was God's providence and a sign of His provision by divine appointment.

God is always on time; when our hope seems really shattered, then God shows up! Through this He empties us of our own, so that He can give from His resources.

The plan of God for Israel was played out here, through a Moabite woman who had no right to an inheritance in Israel. Neither was Boaz the next of kin required by law to marry Ruth.

The time was now right to play out God's divine purpose. Boaz rose to the challenge of ensuring that proper protocol was adhered to.

Though he was not the next of kin, he was willing to ensure that what belonged rightfully to Naomi was given to her.

Boaz is referred to as a redeemer in the Bible, and there is no one else that has that title of redeemer, except our Lord Jesus, so Boaz was in fact a type or shadow of Christ.

In Ruth 3:12-13 Boaz says,

> "And now it is true that I am a redeemer. Yet there is a redeemer nearer than I. Remain tonight, and in the morning, if he will redeem you, good; let him do it. But if he is not willing to redeem you, then, as the Lord lives, I will redeem you. Lie down until the morning."

Such a transaction would only happen at the gate of the city where the elders gathered. The city gate functioned as a forum for public business, especially in the case of this transaction for redeeming an inheritance.

There was, however, a twist to the whole process, as the relative who had the right to redeem the inheritance was reluctant to do so, since this included him having to take Ruth as a wife. This relative didn't want anything to affect his future inheritance, and so he gave up this right to the next relative in line, which in this case was Boaz.

If only he knew that he would have been in the genealogy of King David and our Saviour Jesus Christ! But this was how God wanted it to be in any case, and of course Boaz completed the whole process in the presence of the elders and witnesses at the gate.

Ruth 4:11 says,

> Then all the people who were at the gate and the elders said, "We are witnesses!"

Boaz therefore became the redeemer for all that belonged to Elimelech, to Chilion and to Mahlon and, of course, Ruth. Boaz thereafter married Ruth, who bore him a son named Obed. Obed was the father of Jesse, who was the father of David and, by virtue of this divine orchestration, part of the genealogy of Jesus.

Despite her nationality, Ruth got everything that she had no right to, as she wasn't an Israelite—but with our God nothing is impossible.

Likewise, with Jesus we all have access to an inheritance that we are not entitled to, but He has given it to us through His shed blood on Calvary.

This redemption at the gate foreshadows our redemption. Hebrews 13:12 says,

> Therefore Jesus also, that He might sanctify the people with His own blood, suffered outside the gate.

Keys to the gate

The most important key to hold for the gates is to know who we are in Jesus. And we are His treasured possession:

> "Now therefore, if you will indeed obey my voice and keep my covenant, you shall be my treasured possession among all peoples, for all the earth is mine; and you shall be to me a kingdom of priests and a holy nation. These are the words that you shall speak to the people of Israel." (Exodus 19:5-6)

As we can see in 1 Peter 2:9, these promises to Israel are also promises to us.

> But you are a chosen race, a royal priesthood, a holy nation, a people for his own possession, that you may proclaim the excellencies of him who called you out of darkness into his marvelous light.

We are a royal priesthood, a people owned by God. If we have this understanding of *whose* we are, it gives us unrestricted access to the throne of God, where we can make decrees and petitions unto our God, as we stand as gatekeepers. It behoves on us as kings and priests to act accordingly in that sphere of authority, which we have as sons of the Most High God.

In 2 Chronicles 20:17 the prophet Jahaziel speaks to Jerusalem besieged by the enemy, outlining an important principle.

> "You will not need to fight in this battle. Stand firm, hold your position, and see the salvation of the Lord on your behalf, O Judah and Jerusalem. Do not be afraid and do not be dismayed. Tomorrow go out against them, and the Lord will be with you."

This by no means implies inaction on our part. We will still need to go to the battlefront, but if we read further, we will see that the Lord already had given an insight and a strategy to the Israelites about the location of their enemy.

They knew supernaturally where the enemy was located; what they didn't know was that the battle had already been won. The prophet Jahaziel says in verse 16,

> "Tomorrow go down against them. Behold, they will come up by the ascent of Ziz. You will find them at the end of the valley, east of the wilderness of Jeruel."

Immediately, Jehoshaphat worshipped and praised God, and he called all Judah and all the inhabitants of Jerusalem to do the same, including the Levites who are gatekeepers by virtue of their role as worshippers.

Gatekeepers must learn to worship and praise God even before the battle. When you learn to praise and worship God as a gatekeeper, He wins the battle for you.

After giving words of encouragement to the people, the king appointed singers who were to sing and praise the Lord, as they went before the army. As soon as they began to sing and praise, the Lord set an ambush against their enemies, and the enemies of Israel destroyed each other.

> And when he had taken counsel with the people, he appointed those who were to sing to the Lord and praise him in holy attire, as they went before the army, and say, "Give thanks to the Lord, for his steadfast love endures forever." And when they began to sing

and praise, the Lord set an ambush against the men of Ammon, Moab, and Mount Seir, who had come against Judah, so that they were routed. For the men of Ammon and Moab rose against the inhabitants of Mount Seir, devoting them to destruction, and when they had made an end of the inhabitants of Seir, they all helped to destroy one another. (2 Chronicles 20:21-23)

To many Christians, praise and worship might seem insignificant. However, we are not operating in the kingdom of man, but in the Kingdom of God. And the Kingdom of God is not subject to man's understanding.

Praise and worship is a very powerful tool in the hands of a gatekeeper!

The final battle has already been won 2,000 years ago. Jesus declared that on the cross.

When Jesus had received the sour wine, he said, "It is finished", and he bowed his head and gave up his spirit. (John 19:30)

The seven cries from the Cross
1. "Father, forgive them" (Luke 23:34)
2. "Today you will be with me" (Luke 23:43)
3. "Dear woman, here is your son" (John 19:26-27)
4. "My God, my God" (Matthew 27:46-47; Mark 15:34-36)
5. "I am thirsty." (John 19:28)
6. "It is finished." (John 19:30)
7. "Father, into your hands" (Luke 23:46)

"It is finished" means that He has accomplished all that the Father wanted Him to, on our behalf. Now, we are fighting from a position of victory and not for victory anymore, because we already have the victory! This revelation is needed, if you want to stand firm and hold your position at the gates.

Passivity is not an option, because there is a fight, but we are resting on the fact that Jesus has already won the battle.

Standing firm at the gates requires us to learn how to pray, praise and worship God, as we see in verse 18 where Jehoshaphat bowed down and worshipped God immediately!

If God has promised it, then He will do it! This should be our mindset.

How do we let God fight for us?

1. Realise that the battle is not ours, but God's.
2. Recognise human limitations, and allow God's strength to work through our fears and weaknesses.
3. Make sure we are pursuing God's interests and not just our own selfish desires.
4. Ask God for help in our daily battles.
5. Take care of the poor.

Proverbs 19:17 says,

> Whoever is generous to the poor lends to the Lord, and he will repay him for his deed.

More often the Church goes to war like defeated soldiers, rather than victorious saints, simply because we are unaware of *whose* we are—our identity—and what our real position is on earth. Sad as though this may be, things don't have to remain that way.

It is time to arise, shine and let the glory of the Lord be upon us. It is time to reflect the glory of God, and show to the world that there is a Kingdom, and that we are representatives of the King.

THE PROBLEM

Now the serpent was more crafty than any other beast of the field that the Lord God had made. He said to the woman, "Did God actually say, 'You shall not eat of any tree in the garden'?" (Genesis 3:10)

Chapter 4

ADAM
THE FIRST GATEKEEPER AND THE
CAUSATIVE EFFECT OF DISOBEDIENCE

Then God said, "Let us make man in our image, after our likeness. And let them have dominion over the fish of the sea and over the birds of the heavens and over the livestock and over all the earth and over every creeping thing that creeps on the earth." So God created man in his own image, in the image of God he created him; male and female he created them. And God blessed them. And God said to them, "Be fruitful and multiply and fill the earth and subdue it, and have dominion over the fish of the sea and over the birds of the heavens and over every living thing that moves on the earth." And God said, "Behold, I have given you every plant yielding seed that is on the face of all the earth, and every tree with seed in its fruit. You shall have them for food. And to every beast of the earth and to every bird of the heavens and to everything that creeps on the earth, everything that has the breath of life, I have given every green plant for food." And it was so. And God saw everything that he had made, and behold, it was very good. And there was evening and there was morning, the sixth day. (Genesis 1:26-31)

MAN WAS CREATED in the image of God, and there was a great blessing bestowed upon him. Adam was given every plant, every tree, every beast, every bird and everything that *"has the breath of life"*.

The Lord breathed into Adam's nostrils the breath of life, so he became a living creature with the ability to carry out his assignments (Genesis 2:7).

Afterwards, He put Adam in charge of the Garden to *"work it and keep it"* (Genesis 2:15). Working it and keeping it was to be the gatekeeper and custodian of the Garden. It was not voluntary, neither was it a part-time job! This was to be his lifetime vocation.

However, even with gatekeepers, there are boundaries, and God rightly gave those boundaries to Adam in Genesis 2:16-17.

> And the Lord God commanded the man, saying, "You may surely eat of every tree of the garden, but of the tree of the knowledge of good and evil you shall not eat, for in the day that you eat of it you shall surely die."

So, Adam had authority over every living thing—on one condition: he should not eat from the tree of the knowledge of good and evil.

Without vision, we will cast off restraint. As gatekeepers, we must stay within the objectives and the remit of our call.

That is an incredible amount of power for anybody! The American President is regarded as the most powerful man on earth, but this is nothing in comparison to the level of influence that was available to man at the time. The world was in the hands of Adam, and he had the freedom to exercise that authority, but within the boundaries given by God. Likewise, we all need some restraint, otherwise we will go beyond our stated assignment.

God had a vision of how it should be, and He clearly gave that to Adam.

> Where there is no prophetic vision the people cast off restraint, but blessed is he who keeps the law. (Proverbs 29:18)

Without vision, we will cast off restraint. As gatekeepers, we must stay within the objectives and the remit of our call.

The apostle Paul says in 1 Corinthians 7:35,

> I say this for your own benefit, not to lay any restraint upon you, but to promote good order and to secure your undivided devotion to the Lord.

Psalm 119:4 says,

You have commanded your precepts to be kept diligently.

Adam was the custodian of everything on earth, and God's intention for him was to be the chief gatekeeper.

Gatekeepers must learn to trust the Lord, and have no other agenda than the Lord's. There is no middle ground or compromise.

Not everyone today, however, is called to be a gatekeeper, though we are all called to pray as believers in the Lord Jesus; in fact we are called to pray without ceasing (1 Thessalonians 5:17).

But for the gatekeeper there is an increased level of responsibility that demands more of us. The Levites, for instance, had been set apart from the twelve tribes of Israel to be priests to the Lord.

The Levites have no portion among you, for the priesthood of the Lord is their heritage. And Gad and Reuben and half the tribe of Manasseh have received their inheritance beyond the Jordan eastward, which Moses the servant of the Lord gave them. (Joshua 18:7)

They had no other assignment but to minister to the Lord in His house.

For the four chief gatekeepers, who were Levites, were entrusted to be over the chambers and the treasures of the house of God. And they lodged around the house of God, for on them lay the duty of watching, and they had charge of opening it every morning. (1 Chronicles 9:26-27)

But with Adam, this was just not an ordinary blessing or calling. It was the full authority that man could ever wield at any given time over God's creation.

Adam named all the living creatures and called them with names according to his own desire (Genesis 2:19-20). This shows the level of trust and fellowship that the Lord wanted to have with man.

Gatekeepers must learn to trust the Lord, and have no other agenda than the Lord's. There is no middle ground or compromise.

If the Lord says, "*Jump!*" don't ask why, just ask the Lord, "*How high?*" There is so much fruit in this when we obey the Lord fully, and not listen to any other voice apart from the Lord's.

Adam lost all of this, because he listened to another voice—the voice of his wife. Please do not take this in a wrong way. There are many times when I have taken the counsel of my wife, and only later on realised the disaster I would have faced, had I not heeded her voice. Those times, it was the Lord speaking through my wife. However, there are times when the Lord speaks to us directly and we have to obey without question.

Listening to voices other than the Holy Spirit's has dire consequences, as has been seen in Adam's case.

Having a praying wife who can hear the voice of the Spirit makes all the difference. If you are not married, I pray that God will give you a godly spouse, as marrying the wrong person could be a snare to your call and destiny.

Adam was given a clear instruction as a gatekeeper, and he had a responsibility to rein his wife in. But in this case he didn't put up any resistance at all.

Genesis 3:6-7 says,

> So when the woman saw that the tree was good for food, and that it was a delight to the eyes, and that the tree was to be desired to make one wise, she took of its fruit and ate, and she also gave some to her husband who was with her, and he ate. Then the eyes of both were opened, and they knew that they were naked. And they sewed fig leaves together and made themselves loincloths.

As a gatekeeper, you cannot and must not be divided in your opinion and question the word of God, because Satan will always come and question you, your spouse, or someone close to you and challenge the word of God. He will always ask, "*Did God actually say?*" You must trust the unchanging word of the unchanging God.

Numbers 23:19 says,

God is not man, that he should lie, or a son of man, that he should change his mind. Has he said, and will he not do it? Or has he spoken, and will he not fulfill it?

Hebrews 13:8 says,

Jesus Christ is the same yesterday and today and forever.

Adam lost a relationship that was full of promises and the goodness of God. It could have been a truly blissful existence, but he listened to another voice!

Listening to voices other than the Holy Spirit's has dire consequences, as has been seen in Adam's case.

The Lord was clearly disappointed with Adam and Eve. The judgement was swift with God judging the Serpent first, then the woman, and eventually the man.

The Lord will make a demand of the words He has spoken to us and judge us based on our obedience to those particular words.

The interesting thing to note is that neither the man nor woman took responsibility for their actions. The woman blamed the Serpent and the man blamed the woman *"that God gave him"*, as if God was also to be blamed for giving him a helpmate. (Genesis 3:13-19)

The Lord will make a demand of the words He has spoken to us and judge us based on our obedience to those particular words.

As gatekeepers, we have to be custodians of the word of God and faithful with whatever the Lord has given into our hands.

The grace of God was manifested once again here, and the Lord clothed Adam and Eve with garments of skins. He sacrificed an animal because without the shedding of blood, there is no redemption (Genesis 3:21).

However, Adam still had to pay for the consequences of his actions, and he was driven from the Garden, with his position as the gatekeeper lost.

A new gatekeeper was appointed to guard the entrance, so man had no access to the Garden.

THE GATEKEEPER

The Lord placed a Cherubim and a flaming sword that turned everywhere to guard the way to the tree of life. (Genesis 3:24)

Lessons to learn from Adam as a gatekeeper:
- Obey the Word of God.
- Listen only to the voice of the Holy Spirit.
- Satan is cunning and will attack your weakest point.
- There are consequences for our sin and disobedience.
- There is grace available.

Chapter 5

LOVING THE PRINCIPLES OF GOD

"Hear, O Israel: The Lord our God, the Lord is one. You shall love the Lord your God with all your heart and with all your soul and with all your might. And these words that I command you today shall be on your heart. You shall teach them diligently to your children, and shall talk of them when you sit in your house, and when you walk by the way, and when you lie down, and when you rise. You shall bind them as a sign on your hand, and they shall be as frontlets between your eyes. You shall write them on the doorposts of your house and on your gates."(Deuteronomy 6:4-9)

THIS SCRIPTURE speaks about many things that are consistent with the commandment to love God with all of our heart and all of our soul and might. In most of our nations today there are many 'gods', and as a gatekeeper you cannot be divided between two opinions regarding to the only true God.

Those who know their God shall be strong and perform mighty deeds, and stand firm, regardless of the schemes of the enemy.

Daniel 11:32 prophesies,

He shall seduce with flattery those who violate the covenant, but the people who know their God shall stand firm and take action.

As gatekeepers, we must always obey God's Word. It is only the grace of God that can help us to do this, as we could sometimes fall asleep at the gates, but by His grace we are able to overcome.

Psalm 121:3-4 says,

He will not let your foot be moved; he who keeps you will not slumber. Behold, he who keeps Israel will neither slumber nor sleep.

Our God neither sleeps nor slumbers. And He wants us to pass on the baton of gatekeeping to the next generation. This is important, as gatekeepers must never be lone rangers, since there is always the danger of being defeated by the enemy if you have no support or backup. You need people who are standing with you at the gates.

Exodus 17:10-13 says,

> So Joshua did as Moses told him, and fought with Amalek, while Moses, Aaron, and Hur went up to the top of the hill. Whenever Moses held up his hand, Israel prevailed, and whenever he lowered his hand, Amalek prevailed. But Moses' hands grew weary, so they took a stone and put it under him, and he sat on it, while Aaron and Hur held up his hands, one on one side, and the other on the other side. So his hands were steady until the going down of the sun. And Joshua overwhelmed Amalek and his people with the sword.

Joshua was the one leading the physical battle against the Amalek, while Moses, Aaron and Hur went up the hill to pray and intercede for Joshua.

Why did Moses need Aaron and Hur?

He could have gone up the hill to pray on his own, as he had done many times, but there was a point when he grew weary.

We can all grow weary at some point, no matter our experience and anointing. In fact, the higher your responsibility and position, the more you need people who will lift up your hands from time to time, and keep them steady until the battle is won.

God has not purposed us to win the battle on our own, but collectively, as His body. Even Jesus was anointed with the Holy Spirit for ministry, so He didn't have to fight on His own.

There have been many casualties of faithful saints who stood on the wall and kept their post, but without any backup, and they grew weary and were exposed to the assault of the enemy. That is why we need to raise a whole generation of gatekeepers, so that we will be able to stand together.

Whatever we allow into the gates of our hearts is what we become. To be effective gatekeepers of our cities and nations, we have to be effective gatekeepers of our hearts and minds. After all, it was King Solomon and his offspring not guarding their hearts that led to the division of Israel and eventually to the downfall of the nation.

Proverbs 4:23 (CJB) says,

> Above everything else, guard your heart; for it is the source of life's consequences.

Everything we do flows from the heart, hence God asks us to love Him with all of our heart.

Deuteronomy 6:18 says,

> And you shall do what is right and good in the sight of the Lord, that it may go well with you, and that you may go in and take possession of the good land that the Lord swore to give to your fathers.

Judges 21:25 says,

> In those days there was no king in Israel. Everyone did what was right in his own eyes.

Because of that, the nation was weak, divided and often oppressed by the neighbouring nations. We will be able possess the gates by doing what is good and right in the eyes of God and walking in unity. But there can be dire consequences when we do what we think is right in our own eyes.

While it is impossible for us to keep everything Jesus asks us to keep, God's grace is more than sufficient; more than outward obedience, He wants us to love Him with our heart.

Jesus has redeemed us from the curse of the Law, so now we are able to follow Him in the power of the Spirit.

> Christ redeemed us from the curse of the law by becoming a curse for us—for it is written, "Cursed is everyone who is hanged on a tree"—so that in Christ Jesus the blessing of Abraham might come to the Gentiles, so that we might receive the promised Spirit through faith. (Galatians 3:13-14)

Our obedience is energised and motivated by the Holy Spirit, and we can be victorious because Jesus has won the victory for us on the cross.

But if there is one area where we have been disobedient, especially when it comes to charismatic Christianity, it is justice and caring for the poor.

Zechariah 7:10 says,

> Do not oppress the widow, the fatherless, the sojourner, or the poor, and let none of you devise evil against another in your heart.

Our obedience is energised and motivated by the Holy Spirit, and we can be victorious because Jesus has won the victory for us on the cross.

Gatekeepers must take heed of the plight of the poor at all times. You will recall that, in the Bible times, the poor, dispossessed, outcasts, the sick and those who needed healing often sat at the gates of the city. If you were a gatekeeper, you were often surrounded by them, so their needs would have been in your mind.

God is not giving us the gates just for ourselves, but for the benefit of the nation. And God will always stand for the weak, the marginalised and the disadvantaged of our society.

How
1. True obedience

> You shall write them on the doorposts of your house and on your gates. (Deuteronomy 11:20)

The laws of God are His principles for life, and they do not negate the grace of God, for grace has set us free to serve God. We need to know the Law. Otherwise, how would I know it is not right to sleep with my neighbour's wife, to steal or commit fornication, and so on? Paul says it very succinctly in Romans 7:7,

What then shall we say? That the law is sin? By no means! Yet if it had not been for the law, I would not have known sin. I would not have known what it is to covet if the law had not said, "You shall not covet."

Psalm 1:1-2 says,

> Blessed is the man who walks not in the counsel of the wicked, nor stands in the way of sinners, nor sits in the seat of scoffers; but his delight is in the law of the Lord, and on his law he meditates day and night.

We must delight ourselves in the Law of the Lord. We must take the principles for life God has given to us seriously. They are for our blessing and protection.

Grace doesn't remove the need for obedience; it makes obedience possible. I'm not referring to sinless perfection; as the apostle Paul teaches, we still need to deal with our flesh, our sinful nature. It is not being legalistic when we take God's instructions to us seriously. I say to you, brethren: delight yourself in the Law of the Lord!

Proverbs 7:1-2 says,

> Keep my commandments and live; keep my teaching as the apple of your eye; bind them on your fingers; write them on the tablet of your heart.

1 Samuel 15:22 says,

> And Samuel said, "Has the Lord as great delight in burnt offerings and sacrifices, as in obeying the voice of the Lord? Behold, to obey is better than sacrifice, and to listen than the fat of rams."

2. Seek justice
Proverbs 21:3 says,

> To do righteousness and justice is more acceptable to the Lord than sacrifice.

Justice must prevail at all times at the gates!

3. Guard your heart

Ecclesiastes 5:1-3 says,

> Guard your steps when you go to the house of God. To draw near to listen is better than to offer the sacrifice of fools, for they do not know that they are doing evil. Be not rash with your mouth, nor let your heart be hasty to utter a word before God, for God is in heaven and you are on earth. Therefore let your words be few. For a dream comes with much business, and a fool's voice with many words.

Proverbs 4:23 says,

> Keep your heart with all vigilance, for from it flow the springs of life.

4. Seek wisdom and understanding

At every step of the way we are confronted with diverse issues, and decisions have to be made. Some can be a matter of life and death; others could potentially change the course of a city or nation. We need wisdom and understanding every day. Without this, our counsel will be called into question, but when we stand and speak at the gate out of the wisdom of God, the world will listen to us.

Proverbs 7:4 (KJV) says,

> Say unto wisdom, "Thou art my sister; and call understanding thy kinswoman"

Proverbs 4:5-7 (NKJV) says,

> Get wisdom! Get understanding! Do not forget, nor turn away from the words of my mouth. Do not forsake her, and she will preserve you; Love her, and she will keep you. Wisdom is the principal thing; therefore get wisdom. And in all your getting, get understanding.

Proverbs 16:16 says,

> How much better to get wisdom than gold! To get understanding is to be chosen rather than silver.

5. Help others grow in discipleship

Luke 6:40 says,

> A disciple is not above his teacher, but everyone when he is fully trained will be like his teacher.

In essence, if you raise disciples for Jesus who are fully trained, they will give you a good covering when you are in the battle. They will be lifting your hands by the power of the Holy Spirit, while you are on the battlefield. And you will do the same for them.

6. Cover your back

You need prayer cover. We do not have to become casualties in spiritual war. But to make it, we need people praying for us and covering us, while we are in the heat of the battle. Having trusted friends who are disciples of Jesus prevents unnecessary casualties.

Chapter 6

THE TRIGGER LINE

"From the days of John the Baptist until now the kingdom of heaven has suffered violence, and the violent take it by force." (Matthew 11:12)

WHO IS STANDING at our gates? Genesis 22:17 makes it abundantly clear that the enemies are at the gates. We have failed to maintain our position at the gates, and it is clear that we are still losing ground. Western nations are being turned over to humanism, gay marriage and three-parent babies being proposed now, as the enemy is uprooting the influence of hundreds of years of Christianity.

Nevertheless, we have an assurance that we will possess the gates of our enemies.

But Satan is not going to let go of what he has stolen simply by us asking nicely. We have to wrestle the gates back by force. This is not a physical battle, and primarily not a political battle, but a spiritual one.

The enemy wants to frame this battle for our society as a conflict between progressivism and reactionaries, but, in fact, the battle is an ancient one. Thousands of years ago, Abraham interceded and stood in the gap for the cities of Sodom and Gomorrah, where many sins were rife. He petitioned the Lord not to destroy them if He could find even ten righteous people, but there were none (Genesis 18:24-33, 19:1-29).

This same battle for our nations has raged for a very long time.

Satan knows that if we dispossess him and take over the gates, we will then be able to fulfil the purposes of God and advance the Kingdom on earth.

So there is a lot of resistance, and it will not be an easy handover of keys. Thankfully, we don't need to be asking Satan for permission.

We have allowed Satan control our society for far too long. The Lord is asking us to possess the gates of our enemies, so that we will be able to bring in the greatest harvest earth has even seen. We can have the authority and empowerment to do this in our generation!

Remember, only sons have a right to an inheritance, and this is the time when the revealing of the sons of God is about to be witnessed.

Paul writes,

> For the creation waits with eager longing for the revealing of the sons of God. (Romans 8:19)

But who are the sons of God?

Earlier, Paul writes,

> For all who are led by the Spirit of God are sons of God. (Romans 8:14)

This is not gender specific and in no way leaves women out. We must wrestle to expand the Kingdom of God and begin to rule and reign as sons and daughters of God.

There have been many evangelistic initiatives that have been unable to take off simply because of lack of finances. For example, people have been unable to go on a mission to the nations to preach the gospel and disciple the nation to bring about a Kingdom change. The necessary possessions and treasures to resource this are at the gates of our cities, and they need to be taken by spiritual force.

We believe the Lord has asked our family to care for Aids orphans around the world. This has been a struggle, but we thank God we are beginning to see a breakthrough, as we start to have an understanding of His provision and how we need to lay hold of it in the Spirit and bind the *"strongman"* first, before we can plunder his house.

Jesus says in Matthew 12:29,

> Or how can someone enter a strong man's house and plunder his goods, unless he first binds the strong man? Then indeed he may plunder his house.

This strongman Jesus refers to is the devil with his troops. To bind the strongman, we need the authority and power of Heaven.

Opening the gates of Heaven

The Bible has two dramatic stories about the opening of Heaven, each of which illustrates gates.

The gates of Heaven are spiritual but their opening can be manifested physically. When they open, you commune with the Lord, and this communion can be manifested physically.

It would not be far-fetched to say that wherever we have the presence of God, it becomes a gateway, where we can hear His voice and Heaven is opened to us.

Jacob's ladder

> Then Jacob awoke from his sleep and said, "Surely the Lord is in this place, and I did not know it." And he was afraid and said, "How awesome is this place! This is none other than the house of God, and this is the gate of heaven." (Genesis 28:16-17)

Jacob saw God above the ladder that took angels up and down from Heaven. He was convinced that, indeed, if this was a place where he had an encounter with God, it marked the beginning of something new and important in his life. God doesn't often just show up visibly, but when He does, it is often very dramatic, explosive, revelatory and ultimately a further proof of His majesty and awesome power.

It would not be far-fetched to say that wherever we have the presence of God, it becomes a gateway, where we can hear His voice and Heaven is opened to us.

57

The scripture highlights that the House of God is also the Gate of Heaven. If only the Church can lay hold of this principle and access all that Heaven has for her, how incredibly awesome would that be?

And in our hearts, there is a gateway to Heaven, as the Holy Spirit resides in us.

Jacob's life was never the same again, as this brought about a change in his life. The covenant was re-enacted for his generation, and he was reminded of what he needed to be and what his true identity was. The Lord reminded Jacob about his inheritance, about the land and the promises of God that had been made to his father and grandfather. There was also the reassurance of God's abiding presence (Gen 28:15).

This is the kind of experience we need to have at the gate, where the Lord is ever present with us. Without Him being with us, we can't even operate at the gate. We need His affirmation and His ever-abiding presence that give us a great confidence in our roles as gatekeepers.

Heaven torn open

In the Gospel of Mark we have a descriptive analysis of the event that occurred after Jesus was baptised.

> And when he came up out of the water, immediately he saw the heavens being torn open and the Spirit descending on him like a dove. (Mark 1:10)

The Bible describes the heaven as being torn open, and this was not just like a tiny door opening in a house. Heaven tore open and out of this opening came a voice that thundered through for everyone to hear. This event was the affirmation of the Son of God and the commissioning of His assignment for the next three and half years.

This was none other than God once again manifesting His power and majesty, not only to Jesus but as a witness to all those that were present at the baptism.

The ministry of Jesus did not start until the opening of the gate of Heaven. He waited thirty years for this event. It was the doorway or what I would call the 'trigger' for everything that was going to happen through Jesus for the next three and a half years of His ministry on earth.

We must be clothed in the righteousness of Jesus to be able to stand against the enemy. But this is not automatic. The Bible clearly instructs us to seek the Kingdom first. Jesus says in Matthew 6:33,

> But seek first the kingdom of God and his righteousness, and all these things will be added to you.

We must seek to live in God's righteousness, and this is ultimately based on His forgiveness. Satan is the accuser of the brethren. He seeks to find faults with us and in us and accuses us before the Father, hence the Bible calls him the accuser. But thank God he has already been defeated!

Revelation 12:10 says,

> And I heard a loud voice in heaven, saying, "Now the salvation and the power and the kingdom of our God and the authority of his Christ have come, for the accuser of our brothers has been thrown down, who accuses them day and night before our God."

The ministry of Jesus did not start until the opening of the gate of Heaven. He waited thirty years for this event. It was the doorway or what I would call the 'trigger' for everything that was going to happen through Jesus for the next three and a half years of His ministry on earth.

Nehemiah's sorrow

Nehemiah (meaning: 'Jehovah comforts') is the central figure of the Book of Nehemiah, which describes his work in rebuilding Jerusalem during the Second Temple period. He was the governor of the Persian Judea under Artaxerxes 1 of Persia.

He was troubled about the news from Jerusalem. Nehemiah 1:3 says,

> And they said to me, "The remnant there in the province who had survived the exile is in great trouble and shame. The wall of Jerusalem is broken down, and its gates are destroyed by fire."

Nehemiah served in the king's court, and he tried to hide his sorrow, but in vain. Nehemiah 2:2-3 says,

> Therefore the king said to me, "Why is your face sad, since you are not sick? This is nothing but sorrow of heart." So I became dreadfully afraid, and said to the king, "May the king live forever! Why should my face not be sad, when the city, the place of my fathers' tombs, lies waste, and its gates are burned with fire?"

Like Nehemiah, every believer should be saddened by the state of his nation. The king's concern gave Nehemiah an opportunity to explain the cause for his sadness, and the king was willing to help Nehemiah.

But although it looked like it was Artaxerxes I that granted Nehemiah his blessing, Nehemiah had been interceding before the living God, and it was his sorrow expressed through intercession before Him that brought the beginning of restoration.

Likewise, even when we want to transform our society, it is the time spent before the living God—in praise, intercession, and in sorrow—that will truly bring about the transformation.

SOLUTION: LAYING HOLD

Chapter 7

THE BEAUTIFUL GATE
ACTS 3:1-10

IN ORDER FOR US to have a full understanding of how we need to proceed with taking back the gates, I'll use the example of the lame man at the Beautiful Gate, which to me is like a picture of the Church today.

There was a man laid at the gate of the Temple called the Beautiful Gate. He had been there from birth and was stationed there to ask for alms from those going into the Temple. This was a very strategic position, as everyone would obviously pass by him and see him. The worshippers going to the Temple would have been the most likely ones to express compassion.

That is why we often see beggars outside church buildings. After all, Jesus once asked a rich man to sell all that he had, give it to the poor and follow Him.

Mark 10:21 says,

> And Jesus, looking at him, loved him, and said to him, "You lack one thing: go, sell all that you have and give to the poor, and you will have treasure in heaven; and come, follow me."

Sometimes, it seems that the beggars know the Bible better than we do!

The lame man was at the Beautiful Gate each day. As a lame man, he wasn't allowed to go into the Temple.

The gate is a place of healing, and the first healing miracle of the Early Church was going to take place at the Beautiful Gate. The significance of it happening at this gate cannot be overemphasised, because the God we serve knows the end from the beginning.

63

The story of the lame man was meant to continue with a beautiful twist, even though he was unaware of this at the time. There was a divine arrangement which God had ordained before he was even born.

Psalm 139:13- 16 says,

> For you formed my inward parts; you knitted me together in my mother's womb. I praise you, for I am fearfully and wonderfully made. Wonderful are your works; my soul knows it very well. My frame was not hidden from you, when I was being made in secret, intricately woven in the depths of the earth. Your eyes saw my unformed substance; in your book were written, every one of them, the days that were formed for me, when as yet there were none of them.

Jesus did only what He saw the Father was doing. Jesus never hurried ahead of the Father. He learned the art of waiting to see what the Father was doing before acting. This is an important lesson for the Church, and for gatekeepers and intercessors.

It could well be that Jesus had passed by this gate several times and had not healed this man. But why? Timing was an essential part of this move of the Holy Spirit through the disciples. One can recognise this theme of time running throughout the ministry of Jesus, even from the first miracle at the Wedding of Cana.

At the wedding, the wine had run out, and Jesus's mother asked Him to do something. John 2:4 says,

And Jesus said to her, 'Woman, what does this have to do with me? My hour has not yet come.'

Jesus did only what He saw the Father was doing. Jesus never hurried ahead of the Father. He learned the art of waiting to see what the Father was doing before acting. This is an important lesson for the Church, and for gatekeepers and intercessors.

John 5:19-20 says,

> So Jesus said to them, "Truly, truly, I say to you, the Son can do nothing of his own accord, but only what he sees the Father doing. For whatever the Father does, that the Son does likewise. For the Father loves the Son and shows him all that he himself is doing. And greater works than these will he show him, so that you may marvel."

When Jesus finally performed His first miracle and turned water into wine at the wedding, it was not only timely; it was the best wine they had ever had.

John 2:10 reports the headwaiter's reaction,

> "Everyone serves the good wine first, and when people have drunk freely, then the poor wine. But you have kept the good wine until now."

The best wine came out and it was never late, just in time. Another instance of timing is the case of Lazarus in Bethany, where Mary and Martha, the sister, felt grieved that Jesus—who was a friend of Lazarus and the family—could have turned up earlier, but He didn't. John 11:6 says about Jesus,

> So, when he heard that Lazarus was ill, he stayed two days longer in the place where he was.

And it was during these two days that Lazarus died. Consequently, many felt resentment.

John 11:37 says,

> But some of them said, "Could not he who opened the eyes of the blind man also have kept this man from dying?"

He could, but it had to be in God's timing, in order to bring glory to the Lord. By the time Jesus came to Bethany, Lazarus had already been buried in a tomb for days, and, normally, at this stage, the body would already be rotting away.

But Jesus said,

"Our friend Lazarus has fallen asleep, but I go to awaken him."
(John 11:11)

Then He went to the tomb. In front of the tomb, He prayed,

"I knew that you always hear me, but I said this on account of the
people standing around, that they may believe that you sent me."
When he had said these things, he cried out with a loud voice,
"Lazarus, come out." The man who had died came out, his hands
and feet bound with linen strips, and his face wrapped with a cloth.
Jesus said to them, "Unbind him, and let him go." (John 11:42-44)

This man at the Beautiful Gate ushered in a new era of the manifest power of God through the apostles. This was a demonstration of what it was going to be like when we call upon the name of Jesus, which invokes the power and the anointing of the Holy Spirit!

Jesus demonstrated the power of God through raising the dead. Only God is able to raise the dead. At the Beautiful Gate God demonstrated that the Church could walk in the delegated authority of Jesus.

This man at the Beautiful Gate ushered in a new era of the manifest power of God through the apostles. This was a demonstration of what it was going to be like when we call upon the name of Jesus, which invokes the power and the anointing of the Holy Spirit!

This was an apostolic miracle, which no one had ever seen before, but it was undeniable, as they had seen the lame man lay daily at the Beautiful Gate since birth!

But Peter said,

"I have no silver and gold, but what I do have I give to you. In the
name of Jesus Christ of Nazareth, rise up and walk!" (Acts 3:6)

What did Peter have? You will recall that the disciples were instructed by Jesus to wait in Jerusalem for the promise of the Father (Acts 1:4-8), to be baptised with the Holy Spirit. What was to ensue afterwards was the receiving of the power that would make them witnesses in all Judea and Samaria, and even to the end of the earth.

The power came on the day of Pentecost, and they were all filled with the promised Holy Spirit. Everyone was able to testify to the mighty works of God, and they spoke in foreign tongues. From then on they all had, not just Peter and John, but all, the power to heal, the power to preach the gospel, and the power to be effective witnesses.

We are not seeing much of that same power in the Church right now. The good news is that the Lord is bringing healing and miracles back to His Church. We are to move in the apostolic anointing, with power, boldness and authority, not as a lame duck that can't impact our society.

The lame man was incapacitated, as he was laid daily at the Beautiful Gate, unable to do anything for himself, therefore unable to fulfil his potential. He had to be carried by relatives or friends to beg at the gate in the morning, and then back wherever he slept in the evening.

We are to move in the apostolic anointing, with power, boldness and authority, not as a lame duck that can't impact our society.

But after his healing the Bible describes him walking, leaping and praising the Lord! And for the first time ever, he was able to go to the Temple. And everyone saw clearly the manifestation of the power of God through the apostles and wanted to hear more. It was a great opportunity not to be missed for Peter to preach, and the crowd listened intently to Peter's sermon, as the once lame man now stood next to him. Five thousand were saved on that day.

In many ways, today's Church is like the lame man at the gates, begging for alms from anyone able to go to the Temple and able to enter God's presence. But Jesus is not coming back for a lame but a glorious bride, so it is time we start to leap and praise His name.

Paul says in Ephesians 5:27,

> So that he might present the church to himself in splendor, without spot or wrinkle or any such thing, that she might be holy and without blemish.

Revelation 22:17 says,

> The Spirit and the Bride say, "Come." And let the one who hears say, "Come." And let the one who is thirsty come; let the one who desires take the water of life without price.

But Jesus is not coming back for a lame but a glorious bride, so it is time we start to leap and praise His name.

We are to maintain this gate of healing with the same authority and power that was shown by Peter and John. This is the gate to the apostolic, and it speaks of God doing a new thing.

Nothing has changed since that time, as God has given that same power and authority to the Church through all ages.

Matthew 10:1 says,

> And he called to him his twelve disciples and gave them authority over unclean spirits, to cast them out, and to heal every disease and every affliction.

At that time, Jesus was still with his disciples, and they were able to do these things only because the Lord was with them in blood and flesh.

But later, Jesus said,

> "Truly, truly, I say to you, whoever believes in me will also do the works that I do; and greater works than these will he do, because I am going to the Father. Whatever you ask in my name, this I will do, that the Father may be glorified in the Son. If you ask me anything in my name, I will do it." (John 14:12)

The Cripplegate

This is not just something that happened in Jerusalem. It is a spiritual principle applicable in all times—even in London.

Cripplegate was one of the Roman London's six gates—the others were Ludgate, Newgate, Aldersgate, Bishopsgate and Aldgate.

John Stow, the historian who wrote *A Survey of London*, published in 1598, quotes a history of Edmund the Martyr, King of the East Angles, by Abbo Floriacensis. It says that in 1010, when the Danes approached Bury St. Edmunds, Bishop Alwyn removed the body of the martyred king to St. Gregory's Church, near St. Paul's. As it passed through Cripplegate, such was the blessed influence it diffused, that many lame persons rose upright, and began to praise God for their miraculous cure.

But this isn't the only amazing story that is linked to the Cripplegate, as Christian meetings at this gate once propelled reformation.

The website *thecripplegate.com* tells how during the Puritan era in London, Baptists and Calvinists alike often found themselves expelled from churches.

For the laypeople the problem that this created was severe, as they were unable to hear the 'full gospel' in churches they attended. Many leaders responded by holding informal gatherings around London. These meetings were relatively small, usually starting at 7am, and they almost always took place in public spaces. They lasted an hour, with the time split between prayer and preaching. Over time, the Cripplegate—one of the most notable gates in London—became the main but unofficial location for what came to be known as the "morning exercises."

The Cripplegate had a consistent leadership, but it also would feature guest appearances from notable men. John Milton, John Foxe, Oliver Cromwell, John Bunyan, Richard Baxter, William Cooper, Stephen Charnock, John Owen, Thomas Manton, Thomas Vincent, Thomas Watson, and Matthew Poole all at some point led the morning exercises at the Cripplegate.

These gatherings ebbed and flowed through the years, and the Cripplegate meetings were at their pinnacle under the reign of Charles II, from 1660 to 1685. But with changing kings and the introduction of relative religious freedom in England, the morning exercises eventually became unnecessary, as the gospel began to return to the churches. Eventually, the Cripplegate's morning exercises were returned to the confines of local churches.

Centuries later, students from the pastors' college led by Spurgeon resurrected the morning exercises. They took to gathering at the Cripplegate before class not only to imitate the morning exercises of the Puritans, but also as a place to discuss and debate contemporary issues in theology. Unfortunately, the Cripplegate was destroyed by German bombing in WWll, but we can see how reformation was maintained and advanced at the gates of London.

When the Church stops walking in the apostolic power, it also loses her ability and power to take over the rest of the gates.

Sadly, today the Church is not in permanent possession of these gates of healing, miracles and breakthroughs because of sin, unbelief and disobedience to our call.

Many ministers start off very well, but later on, they begin to serve their own ministry rather than God. This is similar to what took place in the church of Ephesus in Revelation 2:4 (AMP),

> "But l have this [one charge to make] against you: that you have left (abandoned) the love that you had at first [you have deserted Me, your first love]."

When the Church stops walking in the apostolic power, it also loses her ability and power to take over the rest of the gates.

How

Nehemiah's story gives us understanding on how to restore our position as gatekeepers. Nehemiah had to start from ground zero. Before he could even get on with the gatekeeping, he had to rebuild the city walls first.

> When Nehemiah heard of the desolation of Jerusalem, he prayed to the God of heaven. (Nehemiah 1:4)

There was genuine repentance with weeping and fasting. Nehemiah was also quick to remind God of the promises He had made to Moses hundreds of years earlier.

> "But if you return to Me, and keep My commandments and do them, though some of you were cast out to the farthest part of the heavens, yet I will gather them from there, and bring them to the place which I have chosen as a dwelling for My name." (Nehemiah 1:9)

The King is willing to help, but we need to know how to approach Him. Nehemiah knew how. He prayed and fasted in sorrow.

The key is that we cannot even begin this important task on our own. Psalm 127 is a very good example of this: as is made clear in the first few verses, unless the Lord does it, the whole exercise is going to be in futility and will ultimately fail. Nehemiah responded by acknowledging the problem first, and then with prayer and confession, before he approached the king.

The problem

> And they said unto me, "The remnant that are left of the captivity there in the province are in great affliction and reproach: the wall of Jerusalem also is broken down, and the gates thereof are burned with fire." (Nehemiah 1:3)

Reflection

> And it came to pass, when I heard these words, that I sat down and wept, and mourned certain days, and fasted, and prayed before the God of heaven. (Nehemiah 1:4)

Petition

This was not a prayer but a petition to the Lord, acknowledging who God is, reaffirming His faithfulness over time and reminding God about His promises concerning the nation of Israel, His chosen people. (Nehemiah 1:5-11)

Confession and repentance

Nehemiah confessed and repented of the sins of the nation, and acknowledged that Israel had acted corruptly and not kept the commandments of the Lord, hence the gates had been burnt down. (Nehemiah 1:6-7)

Approaching the king

Now it was time for Nehemiah to approach the king as a cupbearer, and something happened! The king noticed from the countenance of Nehemiah that he was full of sorrow.

> And the king said to me, "Why is your face sad, seeing you are not sick? This is nothing but sadness of the heart." Then I was very much afraid. (Nehemiah 2:2)

Do the gates of your city that lie in ruins sadden you?

This gave Nehemiah an opportunity to explain the cause of his sadness, and of course he got a response from the king, who was willing to help make things better for Nehemiah.

Do the gates of your city that lie in ruins sadden you?

Remember one thing, though; Nehemiah had served the king well to deserve the honour of being asked what would make things better for him.

How is your service to the Lord? How is your worship of the King of Kings? This is a determining factor as to how far you go in times of adversity.

Nehemiah was not in any way presumptuous about anything, but he prayed again.

The king asked Nehemiah, "*What are you requesting?*"

At this moment, Nehemiah did something that most of us don't do in church—he prayed before he responded! We don't know how long he had time to pray, perhaps only a brief moment, but he prayed.

We rely so much on our intellect and human strategy that we sometimes leave God out completely. We must not for one moment think that Nehemiah did not have an idea or even know what he should be requesting from the king, but he chose the right way, as even Jesus did nothing, except what He saw His Father do. Nehemiah was not in any way presumptuous about anything, but he prayed again.

Nehemiah made his requests to the king after he prayed, and I am persuaded that his requests were based on Heaven's agenda and the heart of the Father. He was emboldened by the Lord to ask for all he needed, even a letter from the king to those that actually prevented the rebuilding of the city in the first place. He found favour with the king, as Nehemiah 2:8 says: "*The king granted him all that he asked for*".

> *We need a proper assessment of the condition of the ruins in order to ascertain what needs to be done.*

At this stage, Nehemiah was still alone. But he needed a few trusted and anointed men to start the initial reassessment of their situation.

We need a proper assessment of the condition of the ruins in order to ascertain what needs to be done.

Thereafter, the commission or call—that is, the burden that the Lord has laid upon you—can be announced and, subsequently, willing and able workers recruited to help in carrying out the task. In Nehemiah's day, what was announced made it abundantly clear about the "reproach" of the gates lying in ruins and what was needed to restore them. The rebuilding was to remove the

> *"So we built the wall. And all the wall was joined together to half its height, for the people had a mind to work."*

reproach. There is similarly a reproach in our cities and the gates are likewise burned. But will we volunteer to rebuild and remove the reproach in our cities? That's what the Lord desires.

God needs people who have a mind to work. After Nehemiah arrived in Jerusalem, they began to restore the walls. Nehemiah 4:6 says,

> So we built the wall. And all the wall was joined together to half its height, for the people had a mind to work.

Working hard is the only way to silence those like Sanballat and the Tobiah of Nehemiah's time who will always oppose God's work!

Resources

The most important resource is that the Lord is with us! Jeremiah 1:8 says,

> "Do not be afraid of them, for I am with you to deliver you", declares the Lord.

Set a watch

We have to *set a watch*, as we cannot start the process of rebuilding without watchmen who will stand at the gates against the wiles of the enemy. It is necessary to understand that no work of the Kingdom can be built without persistent prayer. Even when we look at the life of the Early Church that had received the baptism of the Holy Spirit, all they did was based on persistent prayer.

You do not have to physically stand at any gates; this is a position in the Spirit. David applied this principle, even when he was hiding in the desert. Psalm 63 by David says,

> I meditate on You in the night watches. (Psalm 63:6)

He was the leader of his band of warriors, but he would have taken his shift to watch for the enemy through the night, like any soldier. But rather than just watching, he spent this time with the Lord, praying for protection.

You can read all the reports about the state of our society and attempt to act accordingly, but that is not enough without regular, persistent prayer.

We also need encouragers to strengthen our hands, whenever discouragement comes from the enemy. This is not a work you can do on your own.

As we can see in the Book of Nehemiah, rebuilding requires both the sword and the Word!

Those who carried burdens were loaded in such a way that each labored on the work with one hand and held his weapon with the other. (Nehemiah 4:17)

The weapons we need to employ are listed in 2 Corinthians 10:4-6.

For the weapons of our warfare are not of the flesh but have divine power to destroy strongholds. We destroy arguments and every lofty opinion raised against the knowledge of God, and take every thought captive to obey Christ, being ready to punish every disobedience, when your obedience is complete.

Do not forget the needs of the people, while the rebuilding is on-going, as both rebuilding and looking after people must be done together. You must not do one to the exclusion of the other. Get more people on board, as the work progresses.

Volunteers

We are not looking to hire ministers that do all this for money or glory. Only if people volunteer, their hearts are ready.

Thankfully, Psalm 110:3 says,

Your people shall be volunteers in the day of Your power, In the beauties of holiness, from the womb of the morning; You have the dew of Your youth.

Securing the gates

You need to begin to secure the gates by appointing gatekeepers and watchmen, worshippers and priests, to maintain the walls that have been rebuilt.

Nehemiah 7:1-3 says,

Now when the wall had been built and I had set up the doors, and the gatekeepers, the singers, and the Levites had been appointed, I gave my brother Hanani and Hananiah the governor of the castle charge over Jerusalem, for he was a more faithful and God-fearing man than many. And I said to them, "Let not the gates of Jerusalem be opened until the sun is hot. And while they are still standing guard, let them shut and bar the doors. Appoint guards from among the inhabitants of Jerusalem, some at their guard posts and some in front of their own homes."

In our case, we do not often build a physical wall, but operate in the spiritual dimension. That is why watchmen and gatekeepers must have discernment in the Spirit, as otherwise all this activity can become meaningless, with all taking place in an 'invisible realm'— the anointing of the Holy Spirit makes the difference between reality and mere imagination. But we are building spiritual walls that protect us, much like David when he was running away from Saul. He understood that he depended on the invisible protection from the Lord.

Declaration of the word
There will be declarations of the word of the Lord concerning our nations, as that is part of the prophetic function of the Church. We must remember His mercies over us, as the Church has allowed the gates to be burned, and acknowledge our inaction.

In the United Kingdom, secularism, humanism, paganism, other religions and unrighteous laws from our Parliament have transformed our society so much that many don't feel it legitimate to refer to Britain as a Christian nation.

All of these have taken over our gates, and the gates need to be taken back in the Spirit. Over the centuries, the United Kingdom has taken the gospel to the nations and sent missionaries around the world, but this work has been eroded so much that other nations are now sending missionaries to us.

But we are determined to take back the gates, and, personally, I stand as a gatekeeper at Parliament to make intercession, trusting for change at this important gate that determines our laws and how we are governed.

Chapter 8

RELEASING PRAISE AT THE GATES

Make a joyful noise to the Lord, all the earth! Serve the Lord with gladness! Come into his presence with singing! Know that the Lord, he is God! It is he who made us, and we are his; we are his people, and the sheep of his pasture. Enter his gates with thanksgiving, and his courts with praise! Give thanks to him; bless his name! For the Lord is good; his steadfast love endures forever, and his faithfulness to all generations. (Psalm 100)

THE KEY ELEMENT in accessing the throne of God is praise and thanksgiving. There is an unlocking of gates that comes only through offering praise to God. We must consistently have an attitude of praise to enter the gates of God's presence.

Paul and Silas opened the prison gates with praise in Acts 16. Paul and Silas had been jailed, because they had brought deliverance to a slave girl by casting out a demon of divination that was in her. She apparently used this demonic gift to bring much money to her masters. This brought a downturn in the fortunes of her masters, so they seized Paul and Silas and brought them before the rulers, who judged them and subsequently threw them in prison. Their feet were put in chains. But something happened when they started praising the Lord.

About midnight Paul and Silas were praying and singing hymns to God, and the prisoners were listening to them, and suddenly there was a great earthquake, so that the foundations of the prison were shaken. And immediately all the doors were opened, and everyone's bonds were unfastened. (Acts 16:25-26)

When the jailer saw that the doors were opened, he almost took his own life, because there were consequences of losing your prisoners. Paul cried out to him with a loud voice so that he would not harm himself. When the jailer turned on the lights and saw that Paul and Silas had not escaped, he not only surrendered his life to Christ, but his entire family received salvation.

Psalm 100 uses the word "*joyful*". David encourages us to make a joyful noise or shout; this is not dependent on our mood or circumstances.

> We are to praise Him simply because He is God and He made us, to declare the sovereignty of God and acknowledge the glory that is due only to Him. We are to serve the Lord with gladness, even when facing difficulties, just like Paul and Silas did.

We have to acknowledge that without Him we are nothing and that He is our Creator, and the only sensible thing to do is to praise and worship Him. He is the Potter and we are the clay. He rules and reigns in the affairs of men, and He always has the final say. We are to be thankful, and give honour to Him and bless His holy name.

The Bible talks about us rejoicing, even when we face trials. James 1:2-4 says,

> Count it all joy, my brothers, when you meet trials of various kinds, for you know that the testing of your faith produces steadfastness. And let steadfastness have its full effect, that you may be perfect and complete, lacking in nothing.

How many of us today consider it joyful when we fall into trials? We are not only admonished to be joyful, but also to remain steadfast. Jesus says in Luke 6:22-23,

> "Blessed are you when people hate you and when they exclude you and revile you and spurn your name as evil, on account of the Son of Man! Rejoice in that day, and leap for joy, for behold, your reward is great in heaven; for so their fathers did to the prophets."

This is Jesus telling us that, even when we are hated, persecuted, excluded and reviled, we should rejoice and even leap for joy. Do we rejoice? Do I rejoice? The answer for most of us would be a resounding no.

The majority of those who rejoice would probably be somewhere in other continents, like Asia—countries such as Malaysia, Indonesia, China, India and so on—because, although they go through unimaginable persecutions, they love the Lord.

Have you ever wondered about the rewards that will come to those who live according to this scripture? I have travelled to a few of these Asian countries, and the persecutions they endure for being Christians are astounding, yet you never find a complaining or a sad believer.

We must rejoice in the Lord through our trials and difficulties by holding on to His promises.

2 Corinthians 1:20 says,

> For all the promises of God find their Yes in him. That is why it is through him that we utter our "Amen" to God for his glory.

As believers, we have to be resolute, no matter what we are going through. The Lord is faithful to His promises. The only issue we must struggle with is that He determines the time for the fulfilment of them.

We must rejoice in the Lord through our trials and difficulties by holding on to His promises.

As a family, we have gone through incredible times of hardship. Yet, we have not lost our joy but have resolutely hung on to the different prophetic promises that have been spoken to us. We have witnessed the incredible hand of God over our lives. It has not always been easy, but our circumstances have not been the determining factor of our actions.

God has used us to pray and give words of knowledge to many barren women, and He has shown us favour in manifesting

79

His power through us, even while we continue to wait on His promises.

I had an incredible experience during a testing time, when God highlighted to me the power of being thankful, even when everything seems bleak. The automatic gearbox of my Mini Cooper broke down, making the car unusable. The warranty had expired, and we couldn't possibly afford to repair or replace the gearbox. This happened at a time when within the space of a month we had about three weddings to attend, one of which was that of one of my nephews, and of two other couples in the church. We had to catch the bus fully decked out in our wedding gear. You can appreciate what that was like, especially for my wife in her hat and shoes, but we were able to have fun—at least, I had fun teasing my wife (no harm done, as we both laughed). The car was out of action for more than six weeks and there was no sight of any sort of funding coming from anywhere.

One morning, I was in the bathroom, and, just before I picked up my toothbrush, I said spontaneously, *"Thank you Lord for the gearbox!"* I had hardly put the toothpaste on my toothbrush when my mobile phone rang, and my wife said that it was the car service centre, as the caller ID was visible. I told her to ignore the call; I had made it clear to the service centre that I couldn't afford to replace the gearbox, as it would set me back with a couple of thousand pounds, plus the workmanship. In my last conversation with them I had told them that I would contact them when I had the money. My plan B was to get rid of the car, as I was determined I was not going to spend that amount of money to repair a car, while our charity, The Father's Blessing had a need for funding. So, my wife did not pick up the phone, but it rang again twenty minutes later. I was really angry and was going to give them a piece of my mind, as I didn't want any pressure from them.

But the caller calmly told me they were going to repair my car for free! I told him this must be a joke, and that I was not in any mood for jokes, as it was too early in the day, but he repeated these exact same words:

"Mr Adeola, we would be willing to repair your car for free. When can you bring it in?"

And he said he would call me back in about thirty minutes to make all the necessary arrangements. He didn't call back in thirty minutes, or at any time that day, and I came to the conclusion that it was exactly as I had expected—he had made a cruel joke on me. I didn't believe this representative of BMW and one of the biggest car dealerships not only in the UK but in Europe. That they could actually offer to replace my gearbox for free, especially as it was not under any warranty, was just too good to be true!

All this while, I had forgotten the spontaneous thanks I had given for receiving the gearbox. This thanksgiving must have been initiated by the Holy Spirit, as I had no idea where to get it from. I acted like the Syrian General Naaman, who had an expectation of how Elisha was going to heal him, and it was certainly not by bathing in the Jordan River, which happened to be the dirtiest river in the whole region.

But my car was taken in, the gearbox replaced with a new one, and, in the process, a few other faults were discovered. I was given a call to ask whether I wanted these extra repairs carried out, and I immediately said no, but the repairman said this was also going to be free—including replacing the battery that had run flat whilst the car was off the road!

All I had to pay was a voluntary charge for workmanship, so I could have a warranty on the new gearbox. I got a call again the next day after I picked up the car. Of course, my thought was that they had finally come to their senses and wanted their money, but the call was to tell me that they wanted to discount the amount I had paid for the workmanship, and I that I should bring my credit card, so they could make a refund. It was used to purchase four new tires for the car!

God is amazing, and if only we could thank Him and praise Him more, He would do the most amazing things His way—but ultimately for our good!

In Philippians 2:17-18 Paul writes,

> Even if I am to be poured out as a drink offering upon the sacrificial offering of your faith, I am glad and rejoice with you all. Likewise you also should be glad and rejoice with me.

1 Peter 4:13 says,

> But rejoice insofar as you share Christ's sufferings, that you may also rejoice and be glad when his glory is revealed.

We must praise God at all times to enter the presence of God. God delights in our praise and thanksgiving, and He promises to reveal His salvation to us.

Jesus modelled this for us, demonstrating that the giving of thanks releases miracles and answers to prayer. It is about us being able to give thanks before we actually see the answer. It is easier for us to be thankful when we have received an answer to prayers than to be thankful before we receive, as this goes completely against the grain of what we know and what we are used to.

Luke 9:16-17 (AMP) says,

> Then He took the five loaves and the two fish, and He looked up to heaven [and gave thanks] and blessed them, and broke them and kept giving them to the disciples to set before the crowd. They all ate and were [completely] satisfied; and the broken pieces which they had left over were [abundant and were] picked up—twelve baskets full.

The miracle of the five loaves and two fish could only have been possible with the thanksgiving Jesus gave to the Father.

The institution of the Lord's Supper began with thanksgiving, and for us to be able to receive the full benefit that is within the taking of the Communion, we must also give thanks. One important message in this is that we are charged by the Lord to do this as often as we can, in remembrance of Him.

Luke 22:19 says,

> And he took bread, and when he had given thanks, he broke it and gave it to them, saying, "This is my body, which is given for you. Do this in remembrance of me."

The raising of Lazarus is another instance of Jesus modelling thankfulness before receiving.

John 11:40-44 says,

> Jesus said to her, "Did I not tell you that if you believed you would see the glory of God?" So they took away the stone. And Jesus lifted up his eyes and said, "Father, I thank you that you have heard me. I knew that you always hear me, but I said this on account of the people standing around, that they may believe that you sent me." When he had said these things, he cried out with a loud voice, "Lazarus, come out." The man who had died came out, his hands and feet bound with linen strips, and his face wrapped with a cloth. Jesus said to them, "Unbind him, and let him go."

Thanksgiving is, therefore, not only the activation of our faith, but also an assurance that He who has promised is faithful, and we only have to believe!

Psalm 50:23 says,

> The one who offers thanksgiving as his sacrifice glorifies me; to one who orders his way rightly I will show the salvation of God!

How

Jeremiah 7:2-3 says,

> Stand in the gate of the Lord's house, and proclaim there this word, and say, Hear the word of the Lord, all you men of Judah who enter these gates to worship the Lord. Thus says the Lord of hosts, the God of Israel: "Amend your ways and your deeds, and I will let you dwell in this place."

Judah in Hebrew means 'praise', and the tribe of Judah always led any time the children of Israel went to war.

Amend our ways

We have to make a proclamation of praise at the gates, and whenever we want to have access to the courts of our God. However, we must amend our ways by asking God for forgiveness and repenting of all our sins—and He has promised that He will forgive us.

True repentance is a turning away from the error of our ways. Very often we just approach God casually, but Jeremiah 7:3 tells us to amend our ways, and then the Lord will allow us to dwell in His temple.

Many preachers today suggest we should just come as we are, and all will be well—there is no need to change. I'm a firm believer in coming as you are, because where I came from wasn't exactly brilliant, but I'm also a firm believer that we can't remain as we came.

The grace of God accepts us as we are, but it is powerful enough to transform us!

> *Come as you are, but grow up, so you become better in the hands of the One who called you! When we stop growing, we cease to be effective disciples fit for the Master's use.*

Come as you are, but grow up, so you become better in the hands of the One who called you! When we stop growing, we cease to be effective disciples, fit for the Master's use.

We grow by studying the Word of God. We need to change who we spend time with, and be accountable to someone we can trust and who has walked with the Lord longer than we.

We must have a repentant heart before we approach God, and only then can we approach the gates boldly with praise and thanksgiving for all He has done for us.

There is an anointing that comes when we do the right things in the right order. I believe that when we come to know the Lord and submit our lives and our will to Him, we all will have an anointing and boldness from the Holy One in various degrees, as stated in 1 John 2:20, 27.

> But you have been anointed by the Holy One, and you all have knowledge.

Isaiah 45:1-3 says,

> Thus says the Lord to his anointed, to Cyrus, whose right hand I have grasped, to subdue nations before him and to loose the belts of kings, to open doors before him that gates may not be closed: "I will go before you and level the exalted places, I will break in pieces

the doors of bronze and cut through the bars of iron, I will give you the treasures of darkness and the hoards in secret places, that you may know that it is I, the Lord, the God of Israel, who call you by your name."

This verse speaks about the anointing that enabled Cyrus to keep the gates open and for them never to be shut. I believe we can have a similar anointing from the Lord.

There are treasures that are stored up at the gates, and the anointing gives you the authority to enter in and claim all that the Lord has promised. This is a powerful promise that one cannot ignore, as the Lord has done all the clearing of the way for us, and all we need to do is plunder the hidden treasures— which are much more than just finances, but also a wealth of wisdom and all the hidden mysteries of God. A follow-up to this promise that we must also claim at the gates is given in Isaiah 60:11 which says,

There are treasures that are stored up at the gates, and the anointing gives you the authority to enter in and claim all that the Lord has promised.

> Your gates shall be open continually; day and night they shall not be shut, that people may bring to you the wealth of the nations, with their kings led in procession.

When you stand and declare at the gates of praise, they will be opened permanently, because you will have an unhindered access to the King of Kings Himself. Praise is the way to enter into His presence and to access the other gates we want to go through.

Chapter 9

RIGHTEOUSNESS EXALTS A NATION

Open to me the [temple] gates of righteousness; I will enter through them, and I will confess and praise the Lord. This is the gate of the Lord; the [uncompromisingly] righteous shall enter through it. (Psalm 118:19-20, AMP)

AFTER I RECEIVED the prophetic word about writing this book concerning the gates, it soon became obvious to me that the Church has left the city gates to the hands of the enemy.

The Lord highlighted to me Genesis 22:17-18,

"I will surely bless you, and I will surely multiply your offspring as the stars of heaven and as the sand that is on the seashore. And your offspring shall possess the gate of his enemies, and in your offspring shall all the nations of the earth be blessed, because you have obeyed my voice."

I saw that the enemy is having a field day at the gates, and whoever possesses the gates, possesses the city. These thoughts did not leave me, and it was something the Holy Spirit regularly brought to my attention. So, in 2009, when my wife and I led a delegation on a trip to Jerusalem, the theme of that tour was 'Going through the Gates'.

When we arrived in Israel, I met a friend in Jerusalem to whom I spoke to about the gates. He said that I ought to write a book about that. This was confirmation of a prophecy I had received four years earlier—also in Israel. According to the prophecy, there were many books the Lord would be speaking to me about that would benefit the Body of Christ. This word has been spoken to me many times now and is still being spoken today! As this friend was praying for me and encouraging me, the scripture (Psalm 118:19) I had received the day before came back to me.

> Open for me the gates of the righteous; I will enter and give thanks to the Lord.

I believe the Holy Spirit impressed it upon me, as the only way you can speak at the gates with authority is to walk in righteousness.

Our God is holy and, therefore, we ought to walk in holiness. It means walking in the light of the Word—with the help of the Holy Spirit.

Paul says in 2 Corinthians 5:21,

> For our sake he made him to be sin who knew no sin, so that in him we might become the righteousness of God.

Thanks to God, we have His righteousness; that is the only way to be able to stand before the Holy God!

Paul says in Philippians 1:11 that we can be *"filled with the fruit of righteousness that comes through Jesus Christ, to the glory and praise of God."* He says in Romans 3:22 that we have received *"the righteousness of God through faith in Jesus Christ for all who believe. For there is no distinction."*

Through His righteousness, we are able to walk in obedience. This is not legalistic obedience, but obedience that relies on grace. But there is a level of intentionality about it that is often missing in the Church that nowadays often preaches grace as a licence to sin.

Only when we seek God's Kingdom and His righteousness intentionally, will we have the spiritual authority to overcome the enemy at the gates.

Paul writes in 2 Corinthians 5:17:

> Therefore, if anyone is in Christ, he is a new creation; old things have passed away; behold, all things have become new.

In Ephesians 4:24 he asks *"that you put on the new man which was created according to God, in true righteousness and holiness."*

We don't want to put on the old man of sin but the new man of righteousness, because we want to walk with God, and He is holy. Psalm 24:4-6 says,

> He who has clean hands and a pure heart, who does not lift up his soul to what is false and does not swear deceitfully. He will receive blessing from the Lord and righteousness from the God of his salvation. Such is the generation of those who seek him, who seek the face of the God of Jacob. Selah.

Those who live a life that is pleasing to the Lord will be able to exercise the spiritual authority that has been given freely to us. Psalm 29:2 says,

> Give unto the Lord the glory due to His name; worship the Lord in the beauty of holiness.

It therefore behoves on us to give unto the Lord what is due to Him, which is to worship Him in the beauty of His holiness. If you read through the whole psalm, you will notice the benefits of being on the side of the all-powerful God, but these benefits come to us when we serve and worship Him in the beauty of holiness.

There is a road we must walk with the Lord, and it is the highway of holiness.

Isaiah 35:8 says,

> And a highway shall be there, and it shall be called the Way of Holiness; the unclean shall not pass over it. It shall belong to those who walk on the way; even if they are fools, they shall not go astray.

If you have truly been set free from sin, then you want to bear the fruit of holiness, and truly live for God.

Romans 6:22 says,

> But now that you have been set free from sin and have become slaves of God, the fruit you get leads to sanctification and its end, eternal life.

Romans 1:4 says,

> And declared to be the Son of God with power, according to the spirit of holiness, by the resurrection from the dead.

He is the Son, and through Him we have been adopted to the family, and we carry the Spirit of Holiness. You can't have His power without His holiness.

2 Corinthians 5:21 says,

> For our sake he made him to be sin who knew no sin, so that in him we might become the righteousness of God.

It is His righteousness, but it does bring righteousness into our lives. But grace is available to us when we fail. We must learn to come before the Lord as often as we need to. Our imperfection makes us prone to making many mistakes in our walk with God, intentional and unintentional, but there is grace and forgiveness.

But we must extend this forgiveness to others. Hebrews 12:14 tells us that unless we are at peace with all men in holiness, it is impossible to see God "*in holiness*". Are you at peace with your brethren?

Nowadays, we talk a lot about the Spirit but we have no power, and our lives are not a testimony that sets us apart as children of God.

In Acts 1:8, it is written,

> But you will receive power when the Holy Spirit has come upon you, and you will be my witnesses in Jerusalem and in all Judea and Samaria, and to the end of the earth.

Why is the Church lacking in power? One pertinent question we must ask ourselves is, whether our lives reflect the life of our Lord Jesus Christ. Does our life reflect Him in such a way that it is possible for the power of the Holy Spirit to flow out of it?

Many believers today have double or triple lives—church, work and home. They have perfected the art of switching from one mode to the other, like a chameleon, and their church, work and home persons are so different that it nearly amounts to split personality. In the church building, they behave properly, but then they go home to abuse their wife and children! And then they go to the office and behave unethically and dishonestly, as they try to make money. But God sees it all.

> **We cannot stand in a place of spiritual authority, unless our lives reflect Jesus.**

2 Corinthians 3:18 says,

> And we all, with unveiled face, beholding the glory of the Lord, are being transformed into the same image from one degree of glory to another. For this comes from the Lord who is the Spirit.

Brethren, holiness is an indispensable requirement needed to stand at the gates, so that the accuser of the brethren will not have a case against us. If you have any hidden, intentional sins, then you need to come before God, as Satan will point this out to you and remind you that your life is no match for the role of a gatekeeper. But you do have a standing once you come clean with God.

> **God convicts of sin, but He also gives us the power to overcome it through the Holy Spirit.**

Satan, on the other hand, is the master of condemnation and guilt trips. Satan will accuse you when you have failed; you must learn to renew your mind at all times.

Satan *accuses* you of your sin; God *empowers* you against it.

Who is the accuser? The accuser is Satan, and all he does day and night is to rehash your faults and accuse you before the throne of God, because he knows our God is a righteous and just God and, therefore, hates sin. But what he omits is that God is also merciful and that He loves us. Not that God is unaware of our sins and mistakes, but He covers them.

Satan makes it a point of duty to highlight how your behaviour has disqualified you, specifically as a believer, and this ultimately brings condemnation on you. He tells you that you are not qualified to stand in that place and brings discouragement and apathy, and that is often enough for you to give up your call. He heaps condemnation upon you and a sense of guilt, which can ultimately distance you from God, as it makes you feel unworthy. And the devil achieves this primarily through attacking your mind.

In John 8:44 Jesus says of the Pharisees,

> You are of your father the devil, and your will is to do your father's desires. He was a murderer from the beginning, and does not stand in the truth, because there is no truth in him. When he lies, he speaks out of his own character, for he is a liar and the father of lies.

When we fall into any of Satan's traps, we become ineffective in our calling and any role we might be performing in our local assembly.

When we buy in to the lie of Satan's accusation, we forget the grace of God that covers our life.

Your mind becomes a battlefield; rather than thinking of the positive or getting on with the purposes of God for your life, the accusations of Satan become a stumbling block.

The immediate antidote to this accusation is the renewing of our minds. Hebrews 12:2 says,

> Do not be conformed to this world, but be transformed by the renewal of your mind, that by testing you may discern what is the will of God, what is good and acceptable and perfect.

Ephesians 4:23 asks us *"to be renewed in the spirit of your minds."* Romans 8:1-2 says,

> There is therefore now no condemnation for those who are in Christ Jesus. For the law of the Spirit of life has set you free in Christ Jesus from the law of sin and death.

It is this grace that enables us to live holy lives. Unfortunately, holiness is no longer a topic taught from most pulpits, even when the Bible unequivocally encourages us to teach it to the people. Ezekiel 44:23 says,

> And they shall teach My people the difference between the holy and the unholy, and cause them to discern between the unclean and the clean.

Leviticus 10:10-11 says,

> That you may distinguish between holy and unholy, and between unclean and clean, and that you may teach the children of Israel all the statutes which the Lord has spoken to them by the hand of Moses.

What gospel are we teaching today, if we don't teach about the holiness of God? We have filled our pulpits with prosperity and motivational messages, which seem to be the norm, and preach only about one attribute of God. We preach about God as love and dare not mention that He is also the *"consuming fire"*, as referred to in Hebrews 12:29. Also, He is God who judges iniquity.

We don't tell that God hates sin, and hence there is no longer a remorse for our sins. Living the life of a true disciple with accountability is no longer popular.

But true discipleship helps to mentor both new believers and those who have known the Lord longer to walk the straight and the narrow way. But we are more interested in retaining people for the wrong reasons and have become a 'seeker-friendly' movement.

Grace is always available to us when we sin, and this has been paid for, but we must not abuse that for which Christ paid dearly. Romans 6:10-12 says,

> For the death he died he died to sin, once for all, but the life he lives he lives to God. So you also must consider yourselves dead to sin and alive to God in Christ Jesus. Let not sin therefore reign in your mortal body, to make you obey its passions.

2 Corinthians 7:1 (AMP) says,

> Therefore, since these [great] promises are ours, beloved, let us cleanse ourselves from everything that contaminates and defiles body and spirit, and bring [our] consecration to completeness in the [reverential] fear of God.

We must purify ourselves from everything that contaminates us in any way. We do so by constantly allowing the Holy Spirit to direct us and help us live in God's righteousness. Why should we do less?

We need to come back to studying the Word of God. Jesus says in John 17:17,

> Sanctify them in the truth; your word is truth.

We should not become so comfortable with sin that we no longer feel godly sorrow for it.

1 Peter 1:14-16 says,

> As obedient children, do not be conformed to the passions of your former ignorance, but as he who called you is holy, you also be holy in all your conduct, since it is written, "You shall be holy, for I am holy."

James 4:7 says,

> Submit yourselves therefore to God. Resist the devil, and he will flee from you.

We are not able to do any of this on our own, but as we fully submit ourselves and yield our lives to Christ, His grace is able to keep us, and Satan will flee from us.

According to James 4:7, submission to God comes first. This leads to resistance, and eventually the devil will flee.

Romans 3:22 says,

> The righteousness of God through faith in Jesus Christ for all who believe. For there is no distinction.

2 Corinthians 5:21 says,

> For our sake he made him to be sin who knew no sin, so that in him we might become the righteousness of God.

1 Timothy 6:11-12 says,

> But as for you, O man of God, flee these things. Pursue righteousness, godliness, faith, love, steadfastness, gentleness. Fight the good fight of the faith. Take hold of the eternal life to which you were called and about which you made the good confession in the presence of many witnesses.

As you can see, the whole New Testament is full of exhortation to pursue righteousness.

Isaiah 59:2 says,

> But your iniquities have separated you from your God; and your sins have hidden His face from you, so that He will not hear.

If you are to stand in a place of authority at the gates against the enemy, you must be in fellowship with the King who has all the authority.

Things that decrease our spiritual authority

1. Lust of the eyes and pride of possessions

> For all that is in the world—the desires of the flesh and the desires of the eyes and pride of life—is not from the Father but is from the world. (1 John 2:16)

Human desires have been created by God and, therefore, not inherently evil, but they become twisted when they are not submitted to God.

2. Unforgiveness

"But if you do not forgive others their trespasses, neither will your Father forgive your trespasses." (Matthew 6:15)

Jesus gives a startling warning about unforgiveness: if we refuse to forgive others, God will also refuse to forgive us. Why? Because when we don't forgive others, we are denying our common ground as sinners in need of God's forgiveness. God's forgiveness of sin is not the direct result of our forgiving others, but it is based on our realising what forgiveness means (see Ephesians 4:32).

It is easy to ask God for forgiveness, but difficult to grant it to others. Whenever we ask God to forgive us our sin, we should ask if we have forgiven the people who have wronged us.

3. Idolatry

1 Corinthians 10:14 says,

Therefore, my beloved, flee from idolatry.

1 John 5:20-21 says,

And we know that the Son of God has come and has given us understanding, so that we may know him who is true; and we are in him who is true, in his Son Jesus Christ. He is the true God and eternal life. Little children, keep yourselves from idols.

Colossians 3:5 says,

Put to death therefore what is earthly in you: sexual immorality, impurity, passion, evil desire, and covetousness, which is idolatry.

Idolatry is still a serious problem today, though it takes different forms from years gone by. We don't put our trust in statues of wood and stone but in paper money and plastic cards. Putting our trust in anything but God is idolatry. Our modern idols are those symbols of power, pleasure and prestige that we so highly regard. When we understand contemporary parallels to idolatry, Paul's exhortation to *"keep yourselves from idols"* becomes much more meaningful.

4. Prayerlessness
Paul says 1 Thessalonians 5:16-18,

> Rejoice always, pray without ceasing, give thanks in all circumstances; for this is the will of God in Christ Jesus for you.

We cannot spend all our time on our knees, but it is possible to have a prayerful attitude at all times. This attitude is built upon acknowledging our dependence on God, realising His presence within us, and determining to obey Him fully. Then we will find it natural to pray frequent and spontaneous short prayers. A prayerful attitude is not a substitute for regular times of prayer, but should be an outgrowth of those times.

5. Lack of faith
Hebrews 11:6 says,

> And without faith it is impossible to please him, for whoever would draw near to God must believe that he exists and that he rewards those who seek him.

Jesus says in Matthew 17:20,

> "Because of your little faith. For truly, I say to you, if you have faith like a grain of mustard seed, you will say to this mountain, 'Move from here to there,' and it will move, and nothing will be impossible for you."

If you are facing a problem that seems as big and immovable as a mountain, turn your eyes from it and look to Christ for more faith. Only then will you be able to overcome the obstacles that may stand in your way.

6. Adultery and fornication
Proverbs 6:32 says,

> He who commits adultery lacks sense; he who does it destroys himself.

Also, Galatians 5:16-26 is very instructional and helps us to identify the works of the flesh.

> But I say, walk by the Spirit, and you will not gratify the desires of the flesh. For the desires of the flesh are against the Spirit, and the desires of the Spirit are against the flesh, for these are opposed to each other, to keep you from doing the things you want to do. But if you are led by the Spirit, you are not under the law. Now the works of the flesh are evident: sexual immorality, impurity, sensuality, idolatry, sorcery, enmity, strife, jealousy, fits of anger, rivalries, dissensions, divisions, envy, drunkenness, orgies, and things like these. I warn you, as I warned you before, that those who do such things will not inherit the kingdom of God. But the fruit of the Spirit is love, joy, peace, patience, kindness, goodness, faithfulness, gentleness, self-control; against such things there is no law. And those who belong to Christ Jesus have crucified the flesh with its passions and desires. If we live by the Spirit, let us also keep in step with the Spirit. Let us not become conceited, provoking one another, envying one another.

We often feel those evil desires in our hearts, and we can't ignore them. In order for us to follow the Holy Spirit's guidance, we must deal with them decisively. These desires include obvious sins, such as sexual immorality and demonic activities. Those who ignore such sins, or refuse to deal with them, reveal that they have not received the gift of the Spirit that leads to a transformed life. The emphasis on sexual sin may be due to the fact that it is an obvious representative of various kinds of sins; probably it is such a good representative because a person in the throes of sexual temptation easily ignores the consequences, and the results can be destructive.

7. Covetousness
Covetousness places one's ultimate allegiance in the acquisition of the possessions of others, which often leads to other grave sins. "*Put to death*" indicates that Christians have to take severe measures to conquer sin. Watchfulness and prayerfulness against it will be the first steps, with self-discipline following.
Ephesians 5:5 says,

For you may be sure of this, that everyone who is sexually immoral or impure, or who is covetous (that is, an idolater), has no inheritance in the kingdom of Christ and God.

Colossians 3:5 says,

Put to death therefore what is earthly in you: sexual immorality, impurity, passion, evil desire, and covetousness, which is idolatry.

In Matthew 26:41 Jesus says,

"Watch and pray that you may not enter into temptation. The spirit indeed is willing, but the flesh is weak."

Chapter 10

WORSHIP GOD IN SPIRIT AND IN TRUTH

Stand in the gate of the Lord's house, and proclaim there this word, and say, "Hear the word of the Lord, all you men of Judah who enter these gates to worship the Lord. Thus says the Lord of hosts, the God of Israel: 'Amend your ways and your deeds, and I will let you dwell in this place.'" (Jeremiah 7:2-3)

OFTEN, we follow a ritual of worship but maintain a sinful lifestyle. This is religion without any personal commitment to God. We can attend church, take Communion, teach in Sunday school, or sing in the choir—but all of these are empty exercises, unless we are truly doing them for God with a heart of worship. The Lord desires true worshippers who will worship Him in Spirit and in truth!

Jesus says in John 4:23-24,

"But the hour is coming, and is now here, when the true worshippers will worship the Father in spirit and truth, for the Father is seeking such people to worship him. God is spirit, and those who worship him must worship in spirit and truth."

We cannot come to the house of the Lord and worship Him with our filth and sin. God makes clear that we need to amend our ways first.

You cannot go before an earthly monarch without observing the necessary protocol; you'll be marched out by security for breaking it. You could actually be beheaded in some parts of Africa for breaking protocol of how to approach the king! How much more the King of Kings, who is supreme over all things, demands our respect!

God requires us that when we bring our offerings to the altar—this also is an act of worship—and if we have anything against our brother—we need to go and make amends, and then we can come back with our offerings, and only then will our offerings be acceptable to Him.

Jesus is very clear about that in Matthew 5:23-24:

> "So if you are offering your gift at the altar and there remember that your brother has something against you, leave your gift there before the altar and go. First be reconciled to your brother, and then come and offer your gift."

Sin prevents us from entering the gates of worship, and there is no shortcut, but we must make proper restitution.

In Jeremiah 7:5-7 (KJV) God says,

> "For if ye thoroughly amend your ways and your doings; if ye thoroughly execute judgment between a man and his neighbour; If ye oppress not the stranger, the fatherless, and the widow, and shed not innocent blood in this place, neither walk after other gods to your hurt: Then will I cause you to dwell in this place, in the land that I gave to your fathers, forever and ever."

These verses continue by highlighting the different things we need to sort out before we come to worship:

1. Amend your ways
Get rid of sin and be repentant.

2. Love your neighbour
Your neighbours are not just those who live next door or share an apartment with you, but any people who need your help. You help them in a practical way by meeting their needs, as much as the Lord allows you. Your neighbour is someone to whom you are to show mercy (Luke 10:29-37).

3. Do not oppress the strangers but protect them
Take care of widows and the fatherless. This is God's call to every Christian, and it is non-negotiable.

4. Do not follow other gods
This is idolatry and should not be condoned. God is a jealous God. We are to worship Him alone.

This list might seem far too demanding, but if we want to come to worship God in Spirit and in truth, then we have no option but to live our lives according to the principles of God.

James lists all of this to us again in James 1:27:

> Pure religion and undefiled before God and the Father is this, to visit the fatherless and widows in their affliction, and to keep himself unspotted from the world.

Loving our neighbours is a commandment. Jesus reminds us of it in Matthew 22:37-40:

> You shall love the Lord your God with all your heart and with all your soul and with all your mind. This is the great and first commandment. And a second is like it: You shall love your neighbor as yourself. On these two commandments depend all the Law and the Prophets.

Thank God for the grace that we have in Christ! Otherwise, we would be under condemnation, when we do not meet these expectations. But we must understand that the faith of Abraham was a journey. Abraham made many mistakes on the way, but he kept walking in the right direction, to the Promised Land, and God helped him in his weakness.

Paul writes in Romans 6:14 about the paradox of grace:

> For sin will have no dominion over you, since you are not under law but under grace.

God's grace gives us the ability to defeat sin in us and empowers us when we are weak.

In 2 Corinthians 12:9 Paul writes,

> But he said to me, "My grace is sufficient for you, for my power is made perfect in weakness." Therefore I will boast all the more gladly of my weaknesses, so that the power of Christ may rest upon me.

How

We must live each day trusting that there is only one Person that can keep us by His grace, and that is the Lord Jesus, who is forever sympathetic with all of our weaknesses, tempted as we are and yet without sin.

Paul writes in Romans 6:15:

> What then? Are we to sin because we are not under law but under grace? By no means!

Hebrews 4:15-16 says,

> For we do not have a high priest who is unable to sympathize with our weaknesses, but one who in every respect has been tempted as we are, yet without sin. Let us then with confidence draw near to the throne of grace, that we may receive mercy and find grace to help in time of need.

God wants us to walk in obedience and come to Him through the gates of worship in Spirit and in truth. It's a daily walk!

Hebrews 12:28-29 says,

> Therefore let us be grateful for receiving a kingdom that cannot be shaken, and thus let us offer to God acceptable worship, with reverence and awe, for our God is a consuming fire.

Gratitude and worship to God are due to Him in light of salvation. Acceptable worship takes into account God's holiness and His position as the Judge to whom alone worship is due.

Giving

Another form of worship is in our giving out of what He has given to us. This should be done not only for the local church but also for charity and, most importantly, for our neighbours.

Let us go through the gates of worship together! You can begin now by putting this book aside for a moment, and going before God, laying all of your cares, worries and issues at His feet, and asking Him with a repentant heart to let you enter His presence through the gates in worship. Do it now!

Golden Gate in the beginning of the 20th century

Chapter 11

GOD'S LOVE FOR THE GATES OF ISRAEL

The Lord loves the gates of Zion more than all the dwellings of Jacob. (Psalm 87:2)

ONE could not possibly write a book on the gates without any mention of Israel—Zion. It would make this exercise incomplete, as everything—whether we like to believe it or not—hinges on our connection with Israel.

The whole task of taking the gates of our cities back is first and foremost about inviting the King of Glory to come in and welcoming Him, before we start to make a claim to anything else available for us at the gates.

Psalm 24:7-10 says,

> Lift up your heads, O gates! And be lifted up, O ancient doors, that the King of glory may come in. Who is this King of glory? The Lord, strong and mighty, the Lord, mighty in battle! Lift up your heads, O gates! And lift them up, O ancient doors, that the King of glory may come in. Who is this King of glory? The Lord of hosts, he is the King of glory! Selah.

Israel is paramount to the function of gatekeepers. You cannot have spiritual authority at the gate if you are anti-Semitic, as this brings a curse. There are so many verses in the Old Testament about God cursing anyone who curses Israel that it is certain that God takes the hatred of Israel seriously. Anti-Semitism is prejudice, hatred or discrimination of Jews as a national, ethnic, religious or racial group. It is a form of racism, and any form of racism is evil, but because of the promises of God for Israel, anti-Semitism also stands in rebellion against specific plans of God.

One wrong view held by many Christians, which is totally contrary to the Word of God, is that God has replaced Israel with the Church because of their disobedience. This is called replacement theology. Or among some theologians, the older and more widely used term is *supersessionism,* since it is said that the Church *supersedes* Israel. Its proponents teach that God has set aside Israel and made the Church the *"new Israel,"* new and improved people of God.

But God has made an everlasting covenant with Israel. Jeremiah 33:20-26 says,

> Thus says the Lord: "If you can break my covenant with the day and my covenant with the night, so that day and night will not come at their appointed time, then also my covenant with David my servant may be broken, so that he shall not have a son to reign on his throne, and my covenant with the Levitical priests my ministers. As the host of heaven cannot be numbered and the sands of the sea cannot be measured, so I will multiply the offspring of David my servant, and the Levitical priests who minister to me." The word of the Lord came to Jeremiah: "Have you not observed that these people are saying, 'The Lord has rejected the two clans that he chose'? Thus they have despised my people so that they are no longer a nation in their sight. Thus says the Lord: If I have not established my covenant with day and night and the fixed order of heaven and earth, then I will reject the offspring of Jacob and David my servant and will not choose one of his offspring to rule over the offspring of Abraham, Isaac, and Jacob. For I will restore their fortunes and will have mercy on them."

Unless there is a change to the "fixed order" of day and night and the heaven and earth, God's covenant with Israel will remain unbroken.

Obviously, that doesn't mean that we can't speak about any wrongs committed by the modern Israel. After all, that is exactly what the Old Testament prophets did in the ancient Israel.

Regardless, there is an everlasting covenant between God and Israel, and the foundation of that covenant is God's faithfulness and not Israel's perfection.

Paradoxically, many Christians apply forgiveness liberally to anyone else but Israel!

Thank God that we are joined now to this covenant as believers in Christ! And God promises that one day, He will transform Israel's relationship with Him.

Jeremiah 32:39-41 says,

Regardless, there is an everlasting covenant between God and Israel, and the foundation of that covenant is God's faithfulness and not Israel's perfection.

"I will give them one heart and one way, that they may fear me forever, for their own good and the good of their children after them. I will make with them an everlasting covenant, that I will not turn away from doing good to them. And I will put the fear of me in their hearts, that they may not turn from me. I will rejoice in doing them good, and I will plant them in this land in faithfulness, with all my heart and all my soul."

Psalm 132:13-18 says,

For the Lord has chosen Zion; he has desired it for his dwelling place: "This is my resting place forever; here I will dwell, for I have desired it. I will abundantly bless her provisions; I will satisfy her poor with bread. Her priests I will clothe with salvation, and her saints will shout for joy. There I will make a horn to sprout for David; I have prepared a lamp for my anointed. His enemies I will clothe with shame, but on him his crown will shine."

You could not possibly stand as a gatekeeper and proclaim God's name, if you hate Zion. Who will hear you?

Psalm 129:5-8 says,

May all who hate Zion be put to shame and turned backward! Let them be like the grass on the housetops, which withers before it grows up, with which the reaper does not fill his hand nor the binder of sheaves his arms, nor do those who pass by say, "The blessing of the Lord be upon you! We bless you in the name of the Lord!"

Isaiah 2:3 says,

> And many peoples shall come, and say: "Come, let us go up to the mountain of the Lord, to the house of the God of Jacob, that he may teach us his ways and that we may walk in his paths." For out of Zion shall go the law, and the word of the Lord from Jerusalem.

We need to connect with Israel to understand the wisdom of God and the fulfilment of all that has been spoken, which points to Zion. Likewise, we need to be in awe—fear of the Lord not fear of the Jews—concerning His covenant people, the Jews.

Isaiah 33:5-6 says,

> The Lord is exalted, for he dwells on high; he will fill Zion with justice and righteousness, and he will be the stability of your times, abundance of salvation, wisdom, and knowledge; the fear of the Lord is Zion's treasure.

Note the wordings of this scripture: *"stability of your times"*, *"abundance of salvation"*, *"wisdom and knowledge"*, and the *"fear of the Lord is Zion's treasure"*!

The Bible states that the Lord roars from Zion i.e. Israel. I wonder who can stand when the Lord roars, especially if you are not on His side!

Joel 3:16-17 says,

> The Lord roars from Zion, and utters his voice from Jerusalem, and the heavens and the earth quake. But the Lord is a refuge to his people, a stronghold to the people of Israel. "So you shall know that I am the Lord your God, who dwells in Zion, my holy mountain. And Jerusalem shall be holy, and strangers shall never again pass through it."

GOD'S LOVE FOR THE GATES

The Lord will always protect Israel, and we are encouraged to pray for the peace of Jerusalem, so that we would prosper.
Psalm 122:6-9 says,

> Pray for the peace of Jerusalem! May they be secure who love you! Peace be within your walls and security within your towers! For my brothers and companions' sake I will say, "Peace be within you!" For the sake of the house of the Lord our God, I will seek your good.

If you want the security of God, it is a commandment to pray for the peace of Jerusalem, and you cannot get it, unless you love her!

Israel is a signpost for the Church in the end-time prophetic timetable.

The Church has a defined role to play concerning Israel, and that is essentially to pray for her and stand as a watchman on the walls of Jerusalem, and give God no rest, until He makes Jerusalem a praise in all the earth.
Isaiah 62:6-7 says,

> "On your walls, O Jerusalem, I have set watchmen; all the day and all the night they shall never be silent. You who put the Lord in remembrance, take no rest, and give him no rest until he establishes Jerusalem and makes it a praise in the earth."

The Lord is there in the name of the gates of the twelve tribes of Israel. Ezekiel 48:31-35 says,

> Three gates, the gate of Reuben, the gate of Judah, and the gate of Levi, the gates of the city being named after the tribes of Israel. On the east side, which is to be 4,500 cubits, three gates, the gate of Joseph, the gate of Benjamin, and the gate of Dan. On the south side, which is to be 4,500 cubits by measure, three gates, the gate of Simeon, the gate of Issachar, and the gate of Zebulun. On the west side, which is to be 4,500 cubits, three gates, the gate of Gad, the gate of Asher, and the gate of Naphtali. The circumference of the city shall be 18,000 cubits. And the name of the city from that time on shall be, The Lord is there.

> The gates give access to the presence of God from all directions. This access prefigures the access to God through Christ, an access extending to all nations.

Revelation 21:12-13 says,

> It had a great, high wall, with twelve gates, and at the gates twelve angels, and on the gates the names of the twelve tribes of the sons of Israel were inscribed—on the east three gates, on the north three gates, on the south three gates, and on the west three gates. And the wall of the city had twelve foundations, and on them were the twelve names of the twelve apostles of the Lamb.

It is very clear to me that the Lord is indeed our gate. This obviously has great significance to the Kingdom and especially to Israel, both today and in the age to come: so how could we possibly not be in alignment with Israel? Scriptures couldn't be clearer on this seemingly thorny issue for some believers.

The Church must align with God's plan; otherwise we are no better than those with the spirit of the Antichrist. If God says He loves Jerusalem or the gates of Zion more than all the dwellings of Jacob (Psalm 87:2), and says this is a chosen place which He desires for Himself, and it is His resting place forever (Psalm 132:13-14), why should we have any problem with the Word of the Lord?

It's time we realign ourselves to the Word of God, so we will prosper, and God can answer us when we pray!

Psalm 105:8-10 says,

> He remembers his covenant forever, the word that he commanded, for a thousand generations, the covenant that he made with Abraham, his sworn promise to Isaac, which he confirmed to Jacob as a statute, to Israel as an everlasting covenant.

According to Zechariah 2:8 and Deuteronomy 32:10, Israel is the apple of God's eye—the most delicate and tender part of the anatomy. That in itself illustrates the tenderness and care He has for Israel.

Gates of Jerusalem

There are ancient gates that are still standing in Jerusalem; they are of utmost significance in the security and protection of the city of Jerusalem.

During the era of the crusader Kingdom of Jerusalem, there were four gates to the Old City, one on each side. The current walls, built by Suleiman the Magnificent, have a total of eleven gates, but only seven are open. Until 1887, each gate was closed before sunset and opened at sunrise. These gates have been known by a variety of names, used in different historic periods and by different ethnic and religious groups.

Open gates
New Gate
Damascus Gate
Herod's Gate
Lions' Gate
Dung Gate
Zion Gate
Jaffa Gate

Sealed gate
Golden Gate

While all these gates now mainly have merely historical value, there is a gate with special significance. This gate is called the Golden Gate, and it is located in the middle of the eastern side of the Temple Mount.

The gate has been permanently sealed, but in Jewish tradition it is believed to be the gate that the Messiah will use when He comes. Ezekiel 44:1-3 (KJV) says,

Then he brought me back the way of the gate of the outward sanctuary which looketh toward the east; and it was shut. Then said the Lord unto me; This gate shall be shut, it shall not be opened, and no man shall enter in by it; because the Lord, the God of Israel, hath entered in by it, therefore it shall be shut. It is for the prince; the prince, he shall sit in it to eat bread before the Lord; he shall enter by the way of the porch of that gate, and shall go out by the way of the same.

Paradoxically, the Ottoman Sultan Suleiman I sealed off the Golden Gate in 1541 to prevent the Messiah's entrance—thus fulfilling the prophecy about the sealed gate! Obviously, he didn't read the Bible well enough!

The Muslims also built a cemetery in front of the gate, in the belief that the precursor to the Messiah, Elijah, would not be able to pass through the Golden Gate, and thus the Messiah would not come. Also, this was because Jewish priests are not permitted to enter a cemetery.

However, the dead will rise when the Messiah comes, so it's of no significance to us.

1 Thessalonians 4:16 says,

> For the Lord himself will descend from heaven with a cry of command, with the voice of an archangel, and with the sound of the trumpet of God. And the dead in Christ will rise first.

The location of the Golden Gate presently points to the prophecy of Zechariah about the Second Coming of Jesus.

Zechariah 14:4-9 says,

> On that day his feet shall stand on the Mount of Olives that lies before Jerusalem on the east, and the Mount of Olives shall be split in two from east to west by a very wide valley, so that one half of the Mount shall move northward, and the other half southward. And you shall flee to the valley of my mountains, for the valley of the mountains shall reach to Azal. And you shall flee as you fled from the earthquake in the days of Uzziah king of Judah. Then the Lord my God will come, and all the holy ones with him. On that day there shall be no light, cold, or frost. And there shall be a unique day, which is known to the Lord, neither day nor night, but at evening time there shall be light. On that day living waters shall flow out from Jerusalem, half of them to the eastern sea and half of them to the western sea. It shall continue in summer as in winter. And the Lord will be king over all the earth. On that day the Lord will be one and his name one.

But why would the Messiah come through a gate? What significance does it have? Obviously, the gate holds a lot of spiritual significance to the Lord, otherwise, why would the Messiah come through it? Kings went in and out of the gates. Jeremiah 17:19 says,

> Thus said the Lord to me: "Go and stand in the People's Gate, by which the kings of Judah enter and by which they go out, and in all the gates of Jerusalem"

In Matthew 24:33 Jesus says, "*So also, when you see all these things, you know that he is near, at the very gates.*"

Jesus was speaking at the very place where Zechariah prophesied He would stand when He comes to establish His Kingdom.

In Matthew 24:33 Jesus says, "So also, when you see all these things, you know that he is near, at the very gates."

The Golden Gate in Jerusalem

Zechariah 14:12-13 prophesied about an end-time battle against Jerusalem.

> And this shall be the plague with which the Lord will strike all the peoples that wage war against Jerusalem: their flesh will rot while they are still standing on their feet, their eyes will rot in their sockets, and their tongues will rot in their mouths. And on that day a great panic from the Lord shall fall on them, so that each will seize the hand of another, and the hand of the one will be raised against the hand of the other.

I want to be on God's side concerning Jerusalem.

How

A gatekeeper must be aligned with God's purposes, as written in the Word of God, and must not be one that is divided between two opinions. This is not a debatable issue, because the only way to stand in a place of authority is to be in complete obedience to the Word of God.

Israel has a definitive role to play in the purposes of God for the Church and the End Times, and we are duty-bound to heed the commandments of God.

A gatekeeper must not engage in anti-Semitism, as this goes against the will of God. It must be understood that the Lord has not renounced Israel and the Jews.

Prejudice against and hatred of Jews has plagued the world for nearly 2,000 years. Early Christian thought held Jews collectively responsible for the crucifixion of Jesus. This religious teaching became embedded in Catholic theology during the first millennium, and later on became part of Protestant theology, with terrible consequences for the Jews.

> History has shown that wherever anti-Semitism has gone unchecked, the persecution of others has been present or not far behind. Defeating anti-Semitism must be a cause of great importance not only for Jews, but for all people who value humanity and justice... (U.S. Department of State, 2008)

Isaiah 42:6-7 says,

> "I am the Lord; I have called you in righteousness; I will take you by the hand and keep you; I will give you as a covenant for the people, **a light for the nations**, to open the eyes that are blind, to bring out the prisoners from the dungeon, from the prison those who sit in darkness." [emphasis mine]

We have to understand that this calling is not dependent on the righteousness of the Jews, but on God's everlasting covenant.

It is not dependent on America, Iran, Hamas, the Palestinians, Britain or any other organisation or nation.

No. The calling of Israel and the Jews as a light for the nations is entirely based on the faithfulness of God and His unchanging attributes.

Israel is Israel, and the Church is the Church. They both have their covenant with God, and God is well able to keep His covenant with both.

MAINTAIN

Religion that is pure and undefiled before God, the Father, is this: to visit orphans and widows in their affliction, and to keep oneself unstained from the world. (James 1:27)

Chapter 12

JUSTICE AT THE GATES

Thus says the Lord: "Go down to the house of the king of Judah and speak there this word, and say, 'Hear the word of the Lord, O king of Judah, who sits on the throne of David, you, and your servants, and your people who enter these gates. Thus says the Lord: "Do justice and righteousness, and deliver from the hand of the oppressor him who has been robbed. And do no wrong or violence to the resident alien, the fatherless, and the widow, nor shed innocent blood in this place. For if you will indeed obey this word, then there shall enter the gates of this house kings who sit on the throne of David, riding in chariots and on horses, they and their servants and their people. But if you will not obey these words, I swear by myself, declares the Lord, that this house shall become a desolation."'" (Jeremiah 22:1-5)

GOD'S COMMAND regarding justice has many facets, which I will discuss in turn.

Orphans and widows
James 1:27 says,

Religion that is pure and undefiled before God, the Father, is this: to visit orphans and widows in their affliction, and to keep oneself unstained from the world.

This scripture deals with:
1. Purity and living a life of holiness.
2. Visiting orphans and widows.

We have dealt a lot with purity and holiness in this book, but one cannot overemphasise that as a gatekeeper, righteousness before God through Christ is vital.

My simple interpretation of James 1:27 is that we cannot profess our faith without meeting the needs of orphans and widows in a very practical way.

We set up a charity in 2007 called The Father's Blessing that seeks to address this issue of James 1:27, but the word the Lord used for us in particular was based on Isaiah 58:6-14. We have embraced this word, and we used the proceeds from the sale of our apartment to start the work in Zambia, Vietnam and to partner with another ministry in Zimbabwe. We are hoping to go to India and Nigeria soon to set up 'Life Centres'.

We have taken on Aids orphans from one of the most Aids-affected communities in Zambia, the Chipata compound, which has the highest incidence of Aids in Zambia. We have adopted these children and care for them and their surviving grandmothers. Two of them, Susan and Rosemary, are in secondary school, and they are the best in their class!

They couldn't speak a word of English only some years ago. We took them from a school in a class of hundred to a private school with a class of twelve and accelerated learning. One of the girls is aspiring to be a pilot, so I guess I need to make more money!

I believe that the Lord sees single mothers also as widows, and as we care for the older widows too, we must not neglect the single mothers, who are in that position for varying reasons, but who are now in Christ. That is the reason for our plans to set up Life Centres in the nations in order to look after them.

This is God's command to us, and we should think carefully on how to meet this basic requirement—which really is nothing more than loving our neighbours as ourselves.

Foreigners

There is a lot of emphasis in Scripture on foreigners. We are to show hospitality to strangers amongst us and really make them feel welcome.

Hebrews 13:1-2 says,

Let brotherly love continue. Do not neglect to show hospitality to strangers, for thereby some have entertained angels unawares.

Our neighbour is anyone that we come across in our daily lives. In the story Jesus told about the Samaritan man (Luke 10:25-36), this was made clear to us, as he helped a complete stranger, whom he had never met before. Those that one would assume should stop and show compassion, the priest and the Levite, did not, which shows how we can easily miss this important aspect of our faith.

How

There are many ways we can bring God's justice to our society, but I will sum this up with Isaiah 58:6-14:

"Is not this the fast that I choose: to loose the bonds of wickedness, to undo the straps of the yoke, to let the oppressed go free, and to break every yoke? Is it not to share your bread with the hungry and bring the homeless poor into your house; when you see the naked, to cover him, and not to hide yourself from your own flesh? Then shall your light break forth like the dawn, and your healing shall spring up speedily; your righteousness shall go before you; the glory of the Lord shall be your rear guard. Then you shall call, and the Lord will answer; you shall cry, and he will say, 'Here I am.' If you take away the yoke from your midst, the pointing of the finger, and speaking wickedness, if you pour yourself out for the hungry and satisfy the desire of the afflicted, then shall your light rise in the darkness and your gloom be as the noonday. And the Lord will guide you continually and satisfy your desire in scorched places and make your bones strong; and you shall be like a watered garden, like a spring of water, whose waters do not fail. And your ancient ruins shall be rebuilt; you shall raise up the foundations of many generations; you shall be called the repairer of the breach, the restorer of streets to dwell in. If you turn back your foot from the Sabbath, from doing your pleasure on my holy day, and call the Sabbath a delight and the holy day of the Lord honorable; if you honor it, not going your own ways, or seeking your own pleasure, or talking idly; then you shall take delight in the Lord, and I will make you ride on the heights of the earth; I will feed you with the heritage of Jacob your father, for the mouth of the Lord has spoken."

There is so much blessing in fulfilling this mandate. We must have a functioning, compassionate ministry to visit orphans and widows in their afflictions. God sees this as a mandate and our 'religion', if I must put it that way.

This simply tells me it is something that has to be done as a necessity. It is not optional, and it must be consistent, so these afflicted ones can see and experience the love of the Father in us and through us.

We are to minister the grace of Jesus to them in a practical way, and not just with words. We must not despise and push out the homeless, the vulnerable and the addicts from our midst.

> We are not in the stage performance business, where a little disturbance in the service must be eliminated by the preacher's personal 'bodyguards'.

Instead, we are supposed to be a loving family for anyone who wants to join us.

Sometimes, we seem to have forgotten of what from and how we have been saved ourselves!

Ephesians 2:8-9 says,

> For by grace you have been saved through faith. And this is not your own doing; it is the gift of God, not a result of works, so that no one may boast.

We must allow the grace of God to abound in all ways to foreigners, orphans and widows—that is God's justice.

Chapter 13

REST (SABBATH)

Then I commanded the Levites that they should purify themselves and come and guard the gates, to keep the Sabbath day holy. Remember this also in my favor, O my God, and spare me according to the greatness of your steadfast love. (Nehemiah 13:22)

THIS IS BY FAR the gate that amazes me the most, as I could have never imagined that there would be any tie between the Sabbath and the gates.

Earlier, in Nehemiah 13:15-16, it says,

In those days I saw in Judah people treading winepresses on the Sabbath, and bringing in heaps of grain and loading them on donkeys, and also wine, grapes, figs, and all kinds of loads, which they brought into Jerusalem on the Sabbath day. And I warned them on the day when they sold food. Tyrians also, who lived in the city, brought in fish and all kinds of goods and sold them on the Sabbath to the people of Judah, in Jerusalem itself.

The gatekeepers apparently had been lax in their duties of maintaining purity as gatekeepers, and they had not bothered to turn up at the gates on the Sabbath. Consequently, no one else thought that keeping the Sabbath was important. Unlike with the rest of Israel, some of the Levites worked on the Sabbath, but it seemed that the only group supposed to work on the Sabbath was the only one that rested! Because the Levites didn't do their work that included reminding the nation of their rest, the nation went on their daily business on the Sabbath, as if it was any other day.

Of course, not every Levite served every Sabbath; hence they also had their Sabbath rest due to the rotation.

This is a warning from the Lord that we cannot be watchmen or gatekeepers without maintaining a lifestyle of rest in God, if we are to help those who are going to be coming through the gates.

The Sabbath as prescribed by God is meant to be a day of rest. It was not really a day to be working or doing any kind of trading, because it was holy to the Lord. But the Levites could work on the Sabbath, because every day was holy for them, as their inheritance was the Lord, and their income came through the Temple.

This is slightly different to us in the New Covenant. The Sabbath rest of the Old Testament was a prophetic promise about the rest we could one day have in the Lord. All days are indeed holy to the Lord, as He himself does not have a day off, and He is God who does not change. When we cease from doing things in our own strength, then we have entered His rest, and not only on the Sabbath, but every day of our lives.

Jesus is Lord of the Sabbath. In essence, this means, that, whenever we refer to the Sabbath, we are referring to the Lord Jesus, and we are to rest in Him. And Jesus set the Sabbath free from the legalism of the Pharisees by performing miracles on the Sabbath and bringing an understanding of what the Sabbath really means.

Even though the Sabbath is very much part of the lives of the Jews in Israel, and Jesus also observed the Sabbath when He walked the earth, nevertheless He taught, healed, and rested on the Sabbath, doing all that the Father wanted him to do.

Mark 3:2-4 says,

> And they watched Jesus, to see whether he would heal him on the Sabbath, so that they might accuse him. And he said to the man with the withered hand, "Come here." And he said to them, "Is it lawful on the Sabbath to do good or to do harm, to save life or to kill?" But they were silent.

The Sabbath is a time when the Word of the Lord is read, heard and taught in the synagogues. We can create that same atmosphere in our lives; all of what transpired with Jesus during the Sabbath could happen also in our own lives.

124

REST (SABBATH)

Jeremiah 17:19-27 (NLT) has one of the many warnings of God concerning the Sabbath.

This is what the Lord said to me: "Go and stand in the gates of Jerusalem, first in the gate where the king goes in and out, and then in each of the other gates. Say to all the people, 'Listen to this message from the Lord, you kings of Judah and all you people of Judah and everyone living in Jerusalem. This is what the Lord says: Listen to my warning! Stop carrying on your trade at Jerusalem's gates on the Sabbath day. Do not do your work on the Sabbath, but make it a holy day. I gave this command to your ancestors, but they did not listen or obey. They stubbornly refused to pay attention or accept my discipline. But if you obey me, says the Lord, and do not carry on your trade at the gates or work on the Sabbath day, and if you keep it holy, then kings and their officials will go in and out of these gates forever. There will always be a descendant of David sitting on the throne here in Jerusalem. Kings and their officials will always ride in and out among the people of Judah in chariots and on horses, and this city will remain forever. And from all around Jerusalem, from the towns of Judah and Benjamin, from the western foothills and the hill country and the Negev, the people will come with their burnt offerings and sacrifices. They will bring their grain offerings, frankincense, and thanksgiving offerings to the Lord's Temple. But if you do not listen to me and refuse to keep the Sabbath holy, and if on the Sabbath day you bring loads of merchandise through the gates of Jerusalem just as on other days, then I will set fire to these gates. The fire will spread to the palaces, and no one will be able to put out the roaring flames.'"

These verses are clear instructions to us concerning the Sabbath, and we can see the blessings (v. 24-26) and the consequences of breaking this commandment (v. 27).

As gatekeepers, we must have times of stillness and rest to hear God. This is our Sabbath, and it must be intentional.

How

The first thing that Nehemiah did was to instruct that the gates be closed on the Sabbath. Nehemiah was not passive. He was someone who took action in respect of every word from God, and every wrong he saw in society. So when Nehemiah saw that the walls of Jerusalem were broken down and the gates had been destroyed by fire, he took steps to deal with it.

Many of us are aware of the broken-down walls and destroyed gates of our nations and have spent much time debating how it happened, why it happened, and how someone else will repair them.

> But have you ever asked yourself whether you are the Nehemiah for your city?

Nehemiah was a man who had a burden for the things of God, and he recognised what was wrong and had the passion to see things put right, on his watch. This should be the attitude of a gatekeeper.

Sometimes, the activities at the gates will seem normal and right, but this is where our discernment kicks in, and we must separate between what seems good and what is godly. People were trading on the Sabbath, and it is easy for us to say we need the money; we need the resources to feed the poor, build more churches and so on. But God knows and is able to meet our needs, and we must learn to follow only the instructions of the King and move only at His word.

One important and consistent requirement is purification. In order to maintain the integrity of our position as gatekeepers, we must sanctify ourselves continually.

There are more promises and blessings for keeping the Sabbath. Isaiah 58:13-14 says,

> "If you turn back your foot from the Sabbath, from doing your pleasure on my holy day, and call the Sabbath a delight and the holy day of the Lord honorable; if you honor it, not going your own ways, or seeking your own pleasure, or talking idly; then you shall take delight in the Lord, and I will make you ride on the heights of the earth; I will feed you with the heritage of Jacob your father, for the mouth of the Lord has spoken."

Hebrews 4:1-11 says,

Therefore, while the promise of entering his rest still stands, let us fear lest any of you should seem to have failed to reach it. For good news came to us just as to them, but the message they heard did not benefit them, because they were not united by faith with those who listened. For we who have believed enter that rest, as he has said, "As I swore in my wrath, 'They shall not enter my rest,'" although his works were finished from the foundation of the world. For he has somewhere spoken of the seventh day in this way: "And God rested on the seventh day from all his works." And again in this passage he said, "They shall not enter my rest." Since therefore it remains for some to enter it, and those who formerly received the good news failed to enter because of disobedience, again he appoints a certain day, "Today," saying through David so long afterward, in the words already quoted, "Today, if you hear his voice, do not harden your hearts." For if Joshua had given them rest, God would not have spoken of another day later on. So then, there remains a Sabbath rest for the people of God, for whoever has entered God's rest has also rested from his works as God did from his. Let us therefore strive to enter that rest, so that no one may fall by the same sort of disobedience.

Our rest is now in Jesus, as He has already accomplished all on the cross, but we must enter that rest intentionally.

The Sabbath is also a day of encouragement and reading of the Scriptures. Acts 13:14-15 says,

But they went on from Perga and came to Antioch in Pisidia. And on the Sabbath day they went into the synagogue and sat down. After the reading from the Law and the Prophets, the rulers of the synagogue sent a message to them, saying, "Brothers, if you have any word of encouragement for the people, say it."

Further reading: Hebrews 8:1-13, Hebrews 12:24, 2 Corinthians 3:6 Exodus 31:15-17, Exodus 35:2.

Sabbath should bring a refreshing. When we rest in the Lord, we cease from our works. It is a refreshing that comes from trusting, just as a child will trust his father.

The rest here is not just a physical rest, which is important, but rest in the assurance that Jesus has accomplished it all.

The Sabbath is not a time of religious exercise, but a time of refreshing, sharing, exhortation, witnessing and works if necessary, as Jesus ministered on the Sabbath.

Should we observe the Sabbath? Certainly, but we should also do all that Jesus did, and that is do the work of Him who sent Jesus.

In John 14:12-14 Jesus says,

> "Most assuredly I say to you, he who believes in me, the works that I do he will do also and greater works than these he will do, because I go to the father."

If Jesus healed on the Sabbath, certainly we are allowed to heal and make the world a better place on the Sabbath!

Chapter 14

THE GATE CHURCH

"And I tell you, you are Peter, and on this rock I will build my church, and the gates of hell shall not prevail against it." (Matthew 16:18)

THIS IS a double-edged word; there is both revelation and an assurance from the Lord. It helps us to know and understand the kind of battle we need not undertake if He has not given us the authority to engage in!

Looking at the context, Jesus was referring to the revelation that Peter had received from the Father about Him as the Son of the Living God. At the same time, He was referring to Himself defending His bride—the Church.

There is no one better equipped to defend the bride than the bridegroom!

Jesus is saying that it is He who will build His Church—not us trying to build His or our church. He's saying, "*I don't need your help, so get on with other things, which I will reveal to you and give you authority to do.*"

Please don't try to do His job!

The next verse in that same chapter talks about the authority that we will be given as followers of Christ, and most importantly, as gatekeepers. As long as we catch the revelation of who He is, we have a sure standing to engage in the warfare by preaching the gospel with signs and wonders following.

Jesus says,

THE GATEKEEPER

"I will give you the keys of the kingdom of heaven, and whatever you bind on earth shall be bound in heaven, and whatever you loose on earth shall be loosed in heaven." (Matthew 16:19)

We have been given the authority to dismantle the works of the evil one. We also have the promise that the gates of hell will never prevail against the Church.

Remember, we are the Church!

> It is sad that we expend so much energy in trying to help Jesus do what He has clearly said He would do Himself.
> The enemy has made us engage in a futile battle that is unnecessary and draining. It is a distraction that keeps us from the main fight.

We need to keep the main thing the main thing and spend more time in bringing the Kingdom to earth, using the keys of authority that we have been given in witnessing, healing the sick and demonstrating the power of the Kingdom.

While the Church of today might not necessarily look, act or seem like the glorious Church we anticipate, it still does behove us not to engage in what we are clearly not authorised to do or have authority for in any way. We have often 'boxed' the Holy Spirit in our services, as the structure and 'order of service' have been a means of asphyxiating the Holy Spirit, hence He's not able to move in our midst.

We have sidelined the prophets, so there are no prophetic checks and balances. Many of the nations do not even welcome the prophets in their midst.

We are to receive the 'keys' of the Kingdom of Heaven to bind and loose, as may be necessary, for the main assignments of the Church.

We are encouraged in Ephesians 4:11-13 to equip the saints for the work of the ministry. This is principally to train them in such a way that they may attain maturity, and be full of faith and the knowledge of Christ.

Ephesians 4:12-16 (KJV) says,

For the perfecting of the saints, for the work of the ministry, for the edifying of the body of Christ: Till we all come in the unity of the faith, and of the knowledge of the Son of God, unto a perfect man, unto the measure of the stature of the fullness of Christ: That we henceforth be no more children, tossed to and fro, and carried about with every wind of doctrine, by the sleight of men, and cunning craftiness, whereby they lie in wait to deceive; But speaking the truth in love, may grow up into him in all things, which is the head, even Christ.

However, there is a degree of tender care and due diligence that a bridegroom has for the bride, which can only be given by the bridegroom, and no one else.

Satan's authority over our lives has been broken, and we must know that we are fighting from the position of victory!

In Luke 10:18-19 Jesus says,

"I saw Satan fall like lightning from heaven. Behold, I have given you authority to tread on serpents and scorpions, and over all the power of the enemy, and nothing shall hurt you."

How

1. Stand in the authority of the Word of God.

2. Stay within the remit of what Jesus has assigned to us, and let Him defend His Church.

3. Know that there are many things the Lord has called us to do as His bride, and that if we focus on that alone, we will bear fruit worthy of the call.

4. Know who you are in Christ! If you have an 'identity crisis'—you are in the constant state of searching for your identity—then you are unable to be an effective gatekeeper.

As a gatekeeper, you must know that your identity is in Christ Jesus.

Paul says in Galatians 2:20,

> I have been crucified with Christ. It is no longer I who live, but Christ who lives in me. And the life I now live in the flesh I live by faith in the Son of God, who loved me and gave himself for me.

This is the way it should be for us—to walk in the fullness of power and authority that we have in Christ Jesus. When you live this way, the only power that will manifest is His only, which means Christ still rules, and you simply live by faith in Christ.

If you know who you are, then there is no fear of what the enemy might do to you, because you already have victory in Christ. This was won for you on the cross of Calvary, and it was costly to the Father. It was a completed work in every respect, and He himself said, "*It is finished*" (John 19:30). There is nothing more to add.

Chapter 15

SPEAKING AT THE GATES

SPEAKING at the gates is when you take a spiritual and positional stand about a burning issue in society with regard to a particular institution or establishment. Speaking at these gates can be both physical and spiritual. You don't have to be physically present to speak at a gate. Your stand or position can be more of a spiritual nature, and that is when you catch the burden, often given by the Lord for that particular situation.

For instance, there might be a law that is being passed in the Houses of Parliament that is deemed ungodly, and you have to take a stand in intercession for this law not to be passed or reversed.

I was once asked whether you have to go to every gate you possibly know, and go and speak and pray at the particular gate. My answer to this important question is yes and no. Sometimes, it is necessary to go and pray at the physical gate, and I do this by going to pray at Parliament and at the front gate of the Prime Minister's residence, which are close to each other. These are very important gates in our nation. However, most of the time you speak at the gates in the Spirit, wherever you are located.

There was a time when the Lord mandated us to go to a particular gateway in Malaysia that is located in Melaka. Melaka is a strategic and international port city. It has a great significance as a gateway into the nation. The colonial masters of the Malacca Sultanate—the British, Dutch, Japanese and the Portuguese—came in to the country to colonise it through this gate.

The Lord gave us Isaiah 62:10 as the mandate to declare and carry it out prophetically:

Go through, go through the gates; prepare the way for the people; build up, build up the highway; clear it of stones; lift up a signal over the peoples.

We had a team of twenty-one volunteers who are leaders, pastors and intercessors, all Malaysians. We arrived in this city and went up St. Paul's Hill where the ruins of St Paul's Church are. It was of one of the earliest churches in Malaysia, built in 1521.

The ruins are located at the summit of the hill, and this became the gate where we spoke by declaring the word of the Lord, coupled with praise, worship and the blowing of the *shofar* intermittently for the next eight hours for Malaysia. Interestingly, there is also a lighthouse located on this hill, and it is still standing.

We acted out Isaiah 62:10 symbolically by removing the old stones and cast these into the sea. We built a 'new highway' with stones from Jerusalem. We anointed the stones, as we laid them on the pathway, and, thereafter, we raised a banner by flying the flags of Malaysia and Israel high right at the entrance of the port, which is still a physical gateway.

We continued speaking at these gates through prayer even after we returned home. The Malaysians continue to stand as gatekeepers for Malaysia.

In an ancient Israeli city, gates were the place where a lot of communication and deliberation took place, and it was where the elders got together and decided on a lot of issues affecting the city, and also regarding individuals. We are reminded of Boaz who took the case of Ruth to the elders at the gate. The decision to give Boaz the right to marry Ruth was decided at the gate, and sealed with an oath. This is also another way of speaking at the gate.

Psalm 127:4-5 says,

Like arrows in the hand of a warrior,
So are the children of one's youth.
Happy is the man who has his quiver full of them;
They shall not be ashamed,
But shall speak with their enemies in the gate.

Speaking at the gates can challenge the people living in the city, and it requires wisdom. Thankfully, not all speaking at the gates needs to be antagonistic.
Proverbs 1:20-22 says,

> Wisdom calls aloud outside;
> She raises her voice in the open squares.
> She cries out in the chief concourses,
> At the openings of the gates in the city
> She speaks her words:
> "How long, you simple ones, will you love simplicity?"

As gatekeepers, our objective is to speak with wisdom that will cut through any foolish talk. For that we need wisdom that has spiritual power. Therefore, gatekeepers must ask for wisdom and understanding to speak God's counsel.
Proverbs 4:7 says,

> The beginning of wisdom is this: Get wisdom, and whatever you get, get insight.

You can't speak wisely, unless you have first acquired wisdom. Thankfully, God is willing to give it to you if you ask Him.

> If any of you lacks wisdom, let him ask of God, who gives to all liberally and without reproach, and it will be given to him. (James 1:5)

Speaking with authority at the gates brings change. A good example is Elisha, who spoke at the gate of Samaria to declare an end to the famine in the land (2 Kings 7:1). At the time, the city was besieged by the Syrians, and people were starving.

It was clearly the word of the Lord through Elisha, and this word came to pass through God striking the Syrians, who left all their food and equipment behind, and fled (2 Kings 7:18).

There is power when the word of the Lord is spoken at the gates. Sometimes, we have to have faith to move with the word of God, like the four lepers in 2 Kings 7:3-11; they approached the Syrian camp in desperation, and found it deserted. Often the most unlikely people are the ones who alert the gatekeepers to take action!

Only those, who hear the word and take the required action, reap the benefits of the word of God.

There has to be a corresponding action when you hear the word of the Lord. The Lord does not just speak through His prophets for the sake of it, but for them to take action in either encouraging the people, or warning them, and sometimes participating in actually helping to move things forward in the fulfilment of that declared word.

At this stage, the prophet released the word, but the gatekeepers needed to bring the word to the king, who at this point had not yet taken any action. Thank God for the four lepers, who heard the word of the Lord and believed it!

Sometimes desperation kicks us into action, as it did for the four lepers. They were not left with many options, as staying in one place had not brought them any sustenance for a considerable period of time. To simply carry on and remain passive was not an option they were even willing to consider, even though all the odds were against them. They had limited options because of their disability and the restrictions that it placed upon them by society.

Oftentimes, the Lord requires us to change location, but because we always want a sign, that spells inaction on our part. Yet when the lepers moved, the Lord was already waiting for them with a large spoil from the camp of the enemy. The Lord had already caused the Syrians to hear the sound of chariots and horses—the sound of a great army—so that they had left all their possessions and fled for their lives. The lepers had a field day carrying off all the spoil, gold and silver, and an abundance of food.

What happened next was that there was desire on the part of the lepers to bring the good news to all the inhabitants of Samaria.

So they went through the right process, which is the most appropriate one for us, and that is, to the gatekeepers.

2 Kings 7:9-11 says,

Then they said to one another, "We are not doing right. This day is a day of good news. If we are silent and wait until the morning light, punishment will overtake us. Now therefore come; let us go and tell the king's household." So they came and called to the gatekeepers of the city and told them, "We came to the camp of the Syrians, and behold, there was no one to be seen or heard there, nothing but the horses tied and the donkeys tied and the tents as they were." Then the gatekeepers were called out, and it was told within the king's household.

They alerted the gatekeepers, who in turn brought this news before the king.

Elisha had spoken the word of the Lord, and this guaranteed a response, but many of us today do not believe the word of the prophets. While this is understandable, as there are many who call themselves prophets but do not in any way represent the Lord, the Bible nevertheless encourages us not to despise prophecy, but to test it. So rather than ignore the prophetic word, put it to the test and check how it aligns with the Word of God.

Paul says in 1 Thessalonians 5:20-21,

Do not despise prophecies, but test everything; hold fast what is good.

2 Peter 1:21 says,

For no prophecy was ever produced by the will of man, but men spoke from God as they were carried along by the Holy Spirit.

1 John 4:1-3 says,

Beloved, do not believe every spirit, but test the spirits to see whether they are from God, for many false prophets have gone out into the world. By this you know the Spirit of God: every spirit that confesses that Jesus Christ has come in the flesh is from God, and every spirit that does not confess Jesus is not from God. This is the spirit of the antichrist, which you heard was coming and now is in the world already.

It must be noted that proclaiming a prophetic word is not a task that is reserved exclusively for prophets or any so-called 'special servants' of God. This is a role that can be carried out by any believing Christian.

Requirements

Zechariah 8:16-17 says,

> "These are the things that you shall do: Speak the truth to one another; render in your gates judgments that are true and make for peace; do not devise evil in your hearts against one another, and love no false oath, for all these things I hate", declares the Lord.

One of the requirements for speaking at the gates is upholding justice—but not necessarily the justice of this world. The justice of God is often not the same as the justice of the world.

The justice of God is about addressing injustice in our society, dealing with homelessness, fighting against 'abortion culture', helping marriages to last, and upholding godly principles in education and the legislative system. These are some of the things God has called us to speak about at the gates.

God's loving attributes desperately need to be expressed in the world today. Through God's Spirit we can show sensitivity to people around us, reflecting God's goodness and honesty to them. You must have a pure heart to stand and speak at the gates, as seen in Zechariah 8:17; God hates false oaths and devising evil, especially when it comes to relationships between believers.

2 Chronicles 23:19 says,

> And he set the gatekeepers at the gates of the house of the Lord, so that no one who was in any way unclean should enter.

Proverbs 14:19 says,

> The evil will bow before the good, and the wicked at the gates of the righteous.

There is a need for understanding as a gatekeeper. The Scripture tells us clearly that we have already won the battle in righteousness, and we know we are the righteousness of God in Christ!

2 Corinthians 5:21 says,

> For He made Him who knew no sin to be sin for us, that we might become the righteousness of God in Him.

Gatekeepers are not fighting a new war. We are simply taking possession of what Jesus has already won by standing at the gates of righteousness. The sinless Saviour took our sins, so we could have God's righteousness.

Elders were the ones who stood at the gates, as this was the place where business was conducted and major decisions were made concerning the city, and today, we need elders to stand in the powerful positions in our cities.

Eldership is not necessarily age-related, but it speaks more of our position in the realm of the Spirit. This is God-given, and you will know or someone in your life—maybe a prophet—will know if you are an elder and able to stand at the gate.

Daniel was a young man but he sat at the gates of the king.

Daniel 2:49 (NKJV) says,

> Also Daniel petitioned the king, and he set Shadrach, Meshach, and Abed-Nego over the affairs of the province of Babylon; but Daniel sat in the gate of the king.

This not for the faint-hearted. Nahum 3:13 says,

> Behold, your troops are women in your midst. The gates of your land are wide open to your enemies; fire has devoured your bars.

The use of *"women"* in this scripture is just a figure of speech for those that are fearful and weak. It certainly does not cast any negative aspersion on women, as many women today are like modern-day Deborahs who are helping the Baraks to awake!

We must also bear in mind that gatekeepers were from the tribe of the Levites. What does this mean for us now? Gatekeepers can't just speak, but they must be worshippers and be people that spend time in the presence of God, for this is where we receive instructions and where we receive strength and power.

There are many people, even Christians, who go to the gates with a real desire to transform society. But without spiritual power and discernment generated in the presence of God, these people soon lose their way.

We are to be in intimacy with the Lord, before we can go out to make declarations and prayers.

Jesus always found time to be alone with God the Father. Luke 6:12 says,

> In these days he went out to the mountain to pray, and all night he continued in prayer to God.

How do we speak at the gates

1. Take counsel

As a gatekeeper, you must learn to take counsel from the Lord at all times. No one battle is the same! Hosea 11:6 says,

> The sword shall rage against their cities, consume the bars of their gates, and devour them because of their own counsels.

You cannot rely on your own counsel, or strategy, as we might call it nowadays. If you do so, you will be doomed.

Unless you make the Lord your counsellor, you will not be able to stand at the gate, as you need Him daily to be effective in this role. Isaiah 50:4-5 says,

> The Lord God has given me the tongue of those who are taught, that I may know how to sustain with a word him who is weary. Morning by morning he awakens; he awakens my ear to hear as those who are taught. The Lord God has opened my ear, and I was not rebellious; I turned not backward.

Like Isaiah, you have to be taught, and you have to incline your ear to hear the Lord, so you know how to open and close the gate each day.

John 5:19 says,

> So Jesus said to them, 'Truly, truly, I say to you, the Son can do nothing of his own accord, but only what he sees the Father doing. For whatever the Father does, that the Son does likewise."

If our Lord Jesus did nothing, except what He saw his Father do, are we not to follow that example?

2. Understand your weapons of warfare
2 Corinthians 10:4-6 (NKJV) says,

> For the weapons of our warfare are not carnal but mighty in God for pulling down strongholds, casting down arguments and every high thing that exalts itself against the knowledge of God, bringing every thought into captivity to the obedience of Christ, and being ready to punish all disobedience when your obedience is fulfilled.

3. Identify the gates of our cities
These are areas such as the parliamentary and local government, education, legal, banking and finance, commerce, the churches, courts, airports, seaports, media and so on.

- Appoint gatekeepers who fit the description given earlier.
- Appoint elders who are to act in an advisory capacity.
- Appoint watchmen and intercessors who will work side by side with the gatekeepers but submit to them.
- Recognise that Jesus is the main Gatekeeper and that, in essence, means victory has already been won! In fact, Jesus is the Gate.
- Fight from a position of victory, with authority. Every gatekeeper must be a person of Ephesians 6, putting on the whole armour of God and being alert. The attributes of Ephesians 6 gatekeepers are that they:
  Put on the whole armour of God.
  Take up the sword, which is the Word of God.
  Understand the enemy—the spiritual forces of evil, rulers, and principalities.
  Stand firm.

Use the shield of faith to extinguish all the fiery darts of the enemy.
Offer all kinds of prayers and supplications.
Keep alert.
Remain in the righteousness of God.

- The Word of God, which is the sword of the Spirit, is the ultimate weapon that needs to be employed at all times. We are clear that no matter what happens, the Word of God stands forever. Isaiah 40:8 says, *"The grass withers, the flower fades, but the word of our God will stand forever."*

  The success of being able to keep the gates depends greatly on the efficacy of the Word of the Lord, and the gatekeeper must recognise this.

- Obey: Genesis 22:18. Wait on the word before you move! We see in Jeremiah that all his actions were predicated only on when the word of the Lord came to him: Jeremiah 32:26, 33:19,23, 34:12, 39:15 are but a few of the verses that show Jeremiah moving only at the word of the Lord.

Paul understood this well. In 2 Timothy 2:9 he says,

> For which I am suffering, bound with chains as a criminal. But the word of God is not bound!

David is also a good example of someone who was never presumptuous, but inquired of the Lord as to how to move and what to do at all times. If you read 2 Samuel 5:19-25, you notice in these verses that even though David was fighting the same enemy again—the Philistines—he still made a separate enquiry about both battles, without presuming to use the same tactics for both. And rightly so, as God gave different strategies in each case.

Discerning of spirits and hearing God are paramount for being a gatekeeper. 1 John 4:1-3 says,

> Beloved, do not believe every spirit, but test the spirits, whether they are of God; because many false prophets have gone out into the world. By this you know the Spirit of God: Every spirit that confesses that Jesus Christ has come in the flesh is of God, and

every spirit that does not confess that Jesus Christ has come in the flesh is not of God. And this is the spirit of the Antichrist, which you have heard was coming, and is now already in the world.

To speak at the gates, you must discern and test the spirits you will be dealing with, as this is vital in making the right judgment.

"These are the things that you shall do: Speak the truth to one another; render in your gates judgments that are true and make for peace; do not devise evil in your hearts against one another, and love no false oath, for all these things I hate," declares the Lord.
(Zechariah 8:16-17)

Chapter 16

WISDOM AND UNDERSTANDING

Blessed is the one who listens to me, watching daily at my gates, waiting beside my doors. (Proverbs 8:34)

IT IS IMPERATIVE that in our assignment as gatekeepers wisdom should be our constant companion. We are not able to stand at the gates if we do not have godly wisdom; otherwise we become a danger to ourselves and others.

God clearly instructs us that we should get wisdom and understanding in Proverbs 4:7 (KJV),

> Wisdom is the principal thing; therefore get wisdom: and with all thy getting get understanding.

Having gone through the Scriptures (specifically Proverbs 8:22-34), we see that wisdom is consistently with God, right from creation. Proverbs 8:22 says,

> The Lord possessed me in the beginning of his way, before his works of old.

The Lord possessed wisdom even before creation, and at every stage of creation, wisdom was at the side of God. It is no wonder that the Lord should highlight the fact that wisdom is a principal thing for the Church to possess.

Every step and every decision of the gatekeeper must be full of wisdom. I say this because quite often the Church engages in battles the Lord has not called us into, and sometimes there are casualties when we step into un-commanded works. We have to engage in battles only within the remit of our call, and there are different levels for each person, hence the need for wisdom. Do you know your calling? Try finding out, and don't let anyone tell you what your calling is. A prophet can only affirm and discern who you are.

We work with wisdom all the time; there must never be a time when we do not engage the services of wisdom.

Wisdom worked with the Lord on a daily basis, and it was indeed a delight to be working alongside wisdom:

> Then I was by him, as one brought up with him: and I was daily his delight, rejoicing always before him. (Proverbs 8:30)

When we are guided by wisdom in our assignments as gatekeepers and even as believers, it becomes a delight, as our decisions are guaranteed to bring the desired result.

The caveat is that we have to follow and abide with the instructions of wisdom, and not neglect it.

Proverbs 8:33 says,

> Hear instruction, and be wise, and refuse it not.

When we listen to instruction, it comes with a blessing, God is glorified and we become effective in our callings.

Proverbs 8:34 says,

> Blessed is the man that heareth me, watching daily at my gates, waiting at the posts of my doors.

Chapter 17

BACK FROM THE DEAD AT THE GATES

Soon afterward he went to a town called Nain, and his disciples and a great crowd went with him. As he drew near to the gate of the town, behold, a man who had died was being carried out, the only son of his mother, and she was a widow, and a considerable crowd from the town was with her. And when the Lord saw her, he had compassion on her and said to her, "Do not weep." Then he came up and touched the bier, and the bearers stood still. And he said, "Young man, I say to you, arise." And the dead man sat up and began to speak, and Jesus gave him to his mother. Fear seized them all, and they glorified God, saying, "A great prophet has arisen among us!" and "God has visited his people!" And this report about him spread through the whole of Judea and all the surrounding country. (Luke 7:11-17)

OFTEN we are at a crossroads at the gate: life has thrown all sorts of slings and arrows at us, and all we can pray and hope for is to meet the Giver of Life at the gate!

The widow of Nain was going through probably the worst time of her life. She had already lost her husband, now her only son was also dead.

Jesus was just coming from what we could describe as a revival! He had just finished healing the centurion's servant with the authority of the word (Luke 7:6-8). A great crowd witnessed the faith of the centurion, who understood what it is to have authority because of his position as a military leader. The centurion simply told Jesus to '*say the word and let my servant be healed*'. He had no doubt in the power and the authority of Jesus. Jesus marvelled at his faith. It was absolute, and when everyone returned to the house, they found the servant to be well, just as he had believed. But the centurion never had an iota of doubt.

The enemies are at the gate, and whenever we stand at the gate we must have that kind of absolute assurance of the authority and power that we possess and carry. We carry the same authority that Jesus carried because the anointing abides in us!

In John 14:12-14 Jesus says,

> "Truly, truly, I say to you, whoever believes in me will also do the works that I do; and greater works than these will he do, because I am going to the Father. Whatever you ask in my name, this I will do, that the Father may be glorified in the Son. If you ask me anything in my name, I will do it."

In 1 John 2:27 Jesus says,

> "But the anointing that you received from him abides in you, and you have no need that anyone should teach you. But as his anointing teaches you about everything—and is true and is no lie, just as it has taught you—abide in him."

There is a lesson to be learnt from this as gatekeepers: authority comes from the faith of God.

You will notice that I didn't speak of having faith in God but of having the *faith of God*. There is a difference which could decide whether you will see what you proclaim at the gate or not see it at all. We all claim to have faith in God, but when we say we have the faith of God, we are talking of His faith, and not our human faith. Both are good, but nothing can beat the faith of God. The centurion had the faith of God: as a man of authority, he understood the *absolute*, which was unquestionable. This is unlike having faith in God, when it is still possible to debate whether God desires to do something or not.

There was a time in my life when I experienced that kind of absolute faith, as the power of God came upon me! There was a pastor friend of mine, who was to travel with a small team and myself to Israel. He had travelled down to Nigeria and was meant to join us on the trip, but he had all kinds of excuses as to why he was not going to be able to make it to Israel that year—and rightly so, as all the 'excuses' were really valid reasons. He had just relocated his family to Nigeria, the container for all the goods was arriving that week, and at that time he still did not have a permanent place for his family to stay. To compound the problem, he developed a terrible and excruciating pain in his legs, such that, even staying in Nigeria, he would probably have not been able to carry out all the tasks he wanted to do. I did not accept his excuses, because I believed that the Lord wanted him to come to Israel, but I still did not get any further word from God as to what to do other than a gentle witness that he was going to make it. I did not call him again about it and left it at that.

On the day I was about to travel, the cab to take me to the airport arrived. I answered the doorbell and went to pick up my luggage. As soon as I picked it up, the power of God came upon me. I was unable to lift my luggage and dropped it, and I heard the Lord say in my spirit, *"Call him to Israel"*, so I called him out by his full name and declared him to drop everything he was doing and start planning to come to Israel. The prayer probably lasted for about two minutes, after which I felt the anointing lifted. This time, as I picked up my luggage, it no longer felt heavy, and I proceeded to the airport and travelled on to Israel. As soon as I got to Israel, the whole team started asking if my friend was coming, and I said yes.

On the second day, I received a call from the pastor saying that he was on his way to Israel, and that he had a stopover in London and would be seeing us soon.

He said that the power of God had come upon him just at the time I had called him to Jerusalem in prayer. He had gone into the kitchen and applied cooking oil to his knees and legs, which became 'anointing oil', and, instantly, he was healed. He booked his flight on the same day and headed to the airport.

This is an authority that came with the faith of God. But it was done in God's own timing, which was the appropriate time. It is vitally important that we move only when the Father moves, and there is great success in that. That was all that Jesus our Master did.

John 5:19-20 says,

> So Jesus said to them, "Truly, truly, I say to you, the Son can do nothing of his own accord, but only what he sees the Father doing. For whatever the Father does, that the Son does likewise. For the Father loves the Son and shows him all that he himself is doing. And greater works than these will he show him, so that you may marvel."

Now let's get back to what happened to the widow of Nain. They met near the gate of the city, and there was a confrontation between the spirit of death and the giver of life, Jesus. Jesus had compassion on the woman. He first consoled her (Luke 7:13), and when He came to touch the casket, everything stood still (Luke 7:14).

You will recall that when Joshua was in a battle, he prayed to the Lord for the sun to stand still. Joshua 10:12-13 says,

> At that time Joshua spoke to the Lord in the day when the Lord gave the Amorites over to the sons of Israel, and he said in the sight of Israel, "Sun, stand still at Gibeon, and moon, in the Valley of Aijalon." And the sun stood still, and the moon stopped, until the nation took vengeance on their enemies. Is this not written in the Book of Jashar? The sun stopped in the midst of heaven and did not hurry to set for about a whole day.

This caused confusion for the enemies, as they could not discern if it was day or night.

Joshua won the battle, because he was in communion with God, who gave him the strategy that brought confusion to the camp of the enemy. When we stand at the gate with the authority of the King and with the anointing that abides in us, everything must stand still, including heaven, while we bring life to that which is dead.

Jesus did not quote any scripture at the time; all he said was, "*Young man I say to you, arise!*"

Let us examine the words "*I say*". That to me is an indication of the anointing on the person of Jesus. He knew He carried authority, which is no different from us today, as we have the same anointing, and He has rightly promised us that we will indeed do greater things. Though some theologians would say we cannot outdo Jesus that is exactly what He wants us—the Church—to do! I do not in any way subscribe to the idea that we are not able to walk in that anointing and power we have been rightly given as born-again, Spirit-filled believers.

Jesus brought life to the gate of the city through that singular act of raising the dead. And immediately after that event, the news spread to the whole region, beyond the city and into the surrounding areas of Judea and Samaria. And there was a great harvest because of this miracle.

We need that same grace and anointing today more than ever.

Gatekeepers must bring life to the gates of our cities, with the authority of the King. If a notable miracle happened at any of our gates, you can be sure the news would spread so fast that many would get to have a real encounter with the living God, and our cities would never be the same again.

It is time to take back the gates of our cities by employing the power of resurrection that has been made available to us, without which we will not experience revival in our cities and nations.

And when the Lord saw her, he had compassion on her and said to her, "Do not weep." Then he came up and touched the bier, and the bearers stood still. And he said, "Young man, I say to you, arise." (Luke 7:13-14)

Chapter 18

JESUS IS THE GATE

"Yes, indeed! I tell you, the person who doesn't enter the sheep-pen through the door, but climbs in some other way, is a thief and a robber. But the one who goes in through the gate is the sheep's own shepherd. This is the one the gate-keeper admits, and the sheep hear his voice. He calls his own sheep, each one by name, and leads them out. After taking out all that are his own, he goes on ahead of them; and the sheep follow him because they recognize his voice. They never follow a stranger but will run away from him, because strangers' voices are unfamiliar to them." Yeshua used this indirect manner of speaking with them, but they didn't understand what he was talking to them about. So Yeshua said to them again, "Yes, indeed! I tell you that I am the gate for the sheep. All those who have come before me have been thieves and robbers, but the sheep didn't listen to them. I am the gate; if someone enters through me, he will be safe and will go in and out and find pasture. The thief comes only in order to steal, kill and destroy; I have come so that they may have life, life in its fullest measure." (John 10:1-10, *Complete Jewish Bible*)

YOU WILL RECALL from an earlier chapter that we had a gatekeeper, Adam, who, due to disobedience, didn't actually do his job the way it should have been carried out. This is a paramount thing every gatekeeper must avoid by all means.

As gatekeepers, we need to understand the fundamentals of these Scripture verses, where Jesus clearly states that He is the Gate. Verse 7 talks about those that have come before and that they are thieves and robbers; it means that the only authentic Gate is Jesus! What better guarantee does any gatekeeper have than having

Jesus as the Gate? This is a profound revelation we need to catch a gatekeepers. This is our confidence in standing at the gates.

And going further, verse 9 speaks about the access we have through the Gate, which is Jesus. You have unlimited access to go through Jesus. There is safety. You can go in and out to find 'pasture', and that is the goodness of the land you are in.

As a gatekeeper, when you stand at the gate, you have to be able to picture Jesus as the Gate, where you have unmitigated access to lay claim to your pasture—goodness, resources, hidden treasures, health, comfort, peace, and so on.

Graham Cooke writes in *The Kind Intentions of God*:

> Jesus is the door into every situation. He is the door into employment. He is the door into health. He is door into healing. He is the door into wholeness. He is the door in every relationship. As you press into Him, space will open up that is designed for you to occupy.

Jesus says in John 14:6,

> "I am the way, and the truth, and the life. No one comes to the Father except through me."

If, indeed, there is one passageway to the Father, and that is through Jesus, then that becomes the Gate.

We often end all of our prayers with the phrase: *In the name of Jesus!* Sometimes as Christians, we do things without actually having a clear understanding why. There is a way to seal all of our prayers and requests to God, and that is the Gate of Jesus. Ephesians 2:18 says,

> For through him we both have access in one Spirit to the Father.

So we have this confidence in coming before the throne of God Hebrews 12:2 says,

> Looking to Jesus, the founder and perfecter of our faith, who for the joy that was set before him endured the cross, despising the shame, and is seated at the right hand of the throne of God.

Jesus is the only way to the Father and the only way we have to gain access to the throne room of God, where we can join with Him on the throne, so we have answers to our prayers.

In John 8:12 Jesus says,

> "I am the light of the world. Whoever follows me will not walk in darkness, but will have the light of life."

But in Matthew 5:14, Jesus says, *"You are the light of the world. A city set on a hill cannot be hidden."* Today, His light shines to the world through us. If we need to find healing, we have to go through Jesus who is our healer. Matthew 9:20-22 says,

> And behold, a woman who had suffered from a discharge of blood for twelve years came up behind him and touched the fringe of his garment, for she said to herself, "If I only touch his garment, I will be made well." Jesus turned, and seeing her he said, "Take heart, daughter; your faith has made you well." And instantly the woman was made well.

Her plight had been heightened by its duration, leaving her hopeless and in an anaemic, weakened condition. Moreover, her haemorrhaging would have made her ceremonially unclean according to Jewish laws, which would have excluded her from normal social and religious relations. And it took determination and guts for her to even think of touching Jesus. But she had a revelation that touching Jesus was the gateway to healing.

And she was healed; her faith made her well.

Jesus is the gate for salvation for the nations, according to Isaiah 9:2:

> The people who walked in darkness have seen a great light; those who dwelt in a land of deep darkness, on them has light shone.

The light of Jesus becomes the gateway for salvation of the nations.

We need the revelation of God to illuminate our path as gatekeepers, and as these scriptures illuminate, Jesus is our light.

When you stand at the gates of your nation and cities, what do you see? Do you see an insurmountable structure in the spirit that overwhelms you so much that you cannot command it to open, or do you see Jesus as the Gate, where you have unhindered access to go through?

If you continually see Jesus as the Gate, then you are able to go through unhindered, so don't go through any other way!

The cross—the ultimate gateway

I want to end this book by bringing focus back on what Jesus did on the cross. It is the cross that enables us to stand as gatekeepers.

One can only imagine the pain that Jesus had to suffer for our redemption. Yet it was the Father's 'pleasure' to crush Him, not because He wanted to cause the Son any pain, but to redeem us. It was the ultimate sacrifice of love for the sins of the world.

> Yet it was the will of the Lord to crush him; he has put him to grief; when his soul makes an offering for guilt, he shall see his offspring; he shall prolong his days; the will of the Lord shall prosper in his hand. (Isaiah 53:10)

Isaiah says that "*the will of the Lord shall prosper in his hand.*" Do we want to prosper in the will of God? Then our complete obedience is paramount regardless of the cost.

And God even tricked Satan, so that Satan thought that he could defeat Jesus on the cross, when it in fact led to God's ultimate victory over Satan.

> None of the rulers of this age understood this, for if they had, they would not have crucified the Lord of glory. (1 Corinthians 2:8)

Even when He could have been released, Jesus made it known to Pontius Pilate that he had no power or the authority to release Him. It says in John 19:10-11 that Pilate said to Him,

> "You will not speak to me? Do you not know that I have authority to release you and authority to crucify you?" Jesus answered him, "You would have no authority over me at all unless it had been given you from above. Therefore he who delivered me over to you has the greater sin."

And in John 10:17-18 Jesus says,

> "For this reason the Father loves me, because I lay down my life that I may take it up again. No one takes it from me, but I lay it down of my own accord. I have authority to lay it down, and I have authority to take it up again. This charge I have received from my Father."

Our heavenly Father in His wisdom made salvation and redemption available to us through the death of His son, Jesus on the Cross of Calvary. We can never quite comprehend the pain and the ultimate price that Jesus Christ had to pay for our salvation and redemption. We are often reminded to bear our cross. Luke 9:23 says,

> And he said to all, "If anyone would come after me, let him deny himself and take up his cross daily and follow me."

But Jesus carried His cross first, and His was a lot heavier than ours.

> So he delivered him over to them to be crucified. So they took Jesus, and he went out, bearing his own cross, to the place called The Place of a Skull, which in Aramaic is called Golgotha. There they crucified him, and with him two others, one on either side, and Jesus between them. (John 19:16-18)

This was part of passing through the gates of Hades, but even the gates of Hades could not stop Him from conquering for us. Acts 2:27 says,

> For you will not abandon my soul to Hades, or let your Holy One see corruption.

In Acts 2:29-31 the apostle Peter says,

> "Brothers, I may say to you with confidence about the patriarch David that he both died and was buried, and his tomb is with us to this day. Being therefore a prophet, and knowing that God had sworn with an oath to him that he would set one of his descendants on his throne, he foresaw and spoke about the resurrection of the

Christ, that he was not abandoned to Hades, nor did his flesh see corruption."

When Jesus died, the curtain of the Temple was torn into two.

> While the sun's light failed. And the curtain of the temple was torn in two. Then Jesus, calling out with a loud voice, said, "Father, into your hands I commit my spirit!" And having said this he breathed his last. Now when the centurion saw what had taken place, he praised God, saying, "Certainly this man was innocent!" (Luke 23:45)

The curtain separated the Holy of Holies from the rest of the Temple, and it has now forever been torn supernaturally from top to bottom to show that God did it, not man.

Ephesians 2:18-22 says,

> For through him we both have access in one Spirit to the Father. So then you are no longer strangers and aliens, but you are fellow citizens with the saints and members of the household of God, built on the foundation of the apostles and prophets, Christ Jesus himself being the cornerstone, in whom the whole structure, being joined together, grows into a holy temple in the Lord. In him you also are being built together into a dwelling place for God by the Spirit.

The gate of Heaven has now been fully opened, and we have unhindered access to the Father through the Son.

> And so, dear brothers and sisters, we can boldly enter heaven's Most Holy Place because of the blood of Jesus. By his death, Jesus opened a new and life-giving way through the curtain into the Most Holy Place. (Hebrews 10:19-20)

We have nothing to fear, as both our sin and death have been defeated on the cross. The ultimate weapon of the gatekeeper is the knowledge that because of what Jesus did on the cross, we have an unobstructed way to the Father.

ABOUT THE FATHER'S BLESSING

TFB or The Father's Blessing was established in 2007 to support and bring hope to orphans and destitute children around the world through education, welfare and healthcare provision. Back when we started, little did we realise of the enormity of the Aids orphans issue. Experts say because the scale of the problem is huge and more prevalent in faraway places, it seems to give cause for inaction. Regardless, orphans are very high on God's agenda of mercy.

The enormity of the problem, coupled with the need to see the eradication of child poverty, has been our main driving force, and, by God's grace, we currently look after ten children in Zambia, twenty-two in Vietnam and one in Israel, and support over twenty-two children through an existing orphanage in Zimbabwe. We expect to take on more children, as more funding comes, but this will only be made possible through people's generous giving.

Here are a few of the things implemented in Vietnam, Zimbabwe and Zambia:

- Vietnam Mission—March 2009
- Wells dug in two villages in Vietnam
- Agape Children Centre adopted in Vietnam where twenty-two children are fed daily and taught to read and write, and skills like sewing, knitting etc.
- Zimbabwe Mission—2010 (Help to support an existing orphanage)
- Ongoing support of Aids orphans in Zambia and their grandmothers and carers.

We could not have achieved any of this without our supporters so we say thank you to everyone who has been involved with TFF in different ways!

Surviving tough times

With the global economic downturn that began some years ago it was tough for many people, which unfortunately meant charity wasn't high on many people's agenda. Charitable giving plummeted and as a charity, we struggled to sign on new supporters, which meant that our level of income nosedived. We experienced major challenges with sustaining commitments and nearly became one of the many charities that did not survive the downturn. Thankfully a handful of our regular givers stepped up and rallied extra support to enable us continue the upkeep of the children in our care, but this was done with great difficulty. Unfortunately, our goal of sponsoring ten more waiting Aids orphans in Zambia has not been achieved yet.

School

The nine children attending a private school in Zambia absolutely love their school, and they are doing remarkably well. They have gone from not being able to speak a word of English to writing and speaking it well and excelling in their classes. Many of them say Maths and English are their favourite subjects, and they all have high ambitions to become professionals. This in itself is a major testimony, as six of them were totally unschooled, when we took on their support and the sponsorship of their education. To see them transformed through the power of education is truly amazing!

The youngest child, four-year-old Maureen, is keen to start school. Her grandmother reports that she cries when her older siblings go to school and often wishes to follow them. She is a bright child and we will have to look at how we can get her into a local nursery school. If you can, please support Maureen!

Health

In 2015, when I visited the children, I learnt that their school attendance was poor, due to ill health. At the time, I prayed for

ABOUT THE FATHER'S BLESSING

them and believed God for their complete healing. I'm delighted to report that in 2016, all except one have had a breakthrough in their health, and their school attendance has greatly improved. In fact, one of the children, Sylvester, who used to suffer from fits, has had his life transformed. He is now quite confident, one of the brightest children in his class, and was recorded as having 100% attendance in school.

Elisha, the one exception, had terrible, bleeding lip sores, that were causing him much pain. He had been to see a doctor and was given medication, but this had not been effective in curing him. We prayed for him to be completely healed and we trusted God for his healing, and to the glory of God, he is now healed completely!

Welfare

All the children are well looked after. To ensure that they continue to thrive at school and at home, we have appointed a family liaison and welfare officer, who will visit the children in their homes to check on their progress and see to any challenges that arise with their schooling and basic needs.

TFB is working in Chipata compound, one of the most deprived communities in Lusaka, supporting and caring for the most vulnerable people—orphans and widows. Thanks to the support of our donors, we are able to sponsor the education of orphaned children, care for their welfare and that of their families, and tackle problems of food poverty and ill health.

Education

Helping to educate children is one of the most effective ways to ensure that they can break out of a cycle of poverty into a future with opportunity. So we sponsor the education of orphaned children, placing them into private schools where we can.

We have had a few successes, and I would like to share some stories of how you have helped make a difference to the lives of orphaned children.

Owen & Botha's story

Rachel, Owen and Botha's grandmother, turned to us when her

daughter died of Aids, leaving her to care for Owen and Botha, aged 7 and 9 years. Rachel was in despair at the loss of her daughter and at the prospect of having to care for her grandchildren with no means to support herself, let alone providing for two young children. She was also terrified that the boys might also have contracted Aids from their mother and would soon pass away. We were able to pray for them for the duration of our time there and the children upon testing were declared HIV-free. Glory to God!

Fighting poverty

We are supporting the most vulnerable people—orphans and widows—through the provision of regular food parcels with essential food items. We are committed to responding to emergency calls for assistance, but know that this is not a permanent solution.

Recently, some of the widows have identified areas of commerce that they wish to engage in, and we are committed in supporting them on the journey to self-sufficiency. Plans are now in place to empower widows to become self-sufficient. Four widows were given micro-finance loans to commence trading activities.

A new chapter

New funding has helped TFB start a new chapter of caring for widowed grandmothers. The funding enables us to support one widowed grandmother. Rhoneia, the oldest and frailest of the grandmothers, would often walk very long distances to look for bottles to sell, so that she could have food to eat for herself and her grandchildren. Often, she would walk miles to get to the TFB team to ask for food.

With the funding received, Rhoneia will be supported to start trading activities to begin on the road to self-sufficiency for herself and her grandchildren.

From sponsoring orphaned children dealing with the loss of their parent to providing food parcels to destitute families, the TFB team in Lusaka helps all those who come to them in desperate need.

If you can, please support our other grandmothers. Your contribution, big or small, will make a real difference.

Project

Our current project is to build a home for the children. Firstly and most importantly, it has been increasingly difficult to give them the level of care they need, because we do not have them presently all under one roof, as they all live with their grandmothers. Also, sadly, we have to report about some of them missing school, as they are sometimes unable to catch the school bus. This is largely due to the long distance they have to cover walking from home, often at the crack of dawn, to the school bus station. We are also concerned about their safety in an environment where rape is rampant.

These children are doing so well in school that we would want them to be regular attendees, and our dream is to improve their quality of lives significantly by having them all under one roof.

Nevertheless, we now have a temporary home for the children and I'm glad to report that two of them, Susan and Rosemary, have now moved to Grade 8 (secondary school) with Susan getting the best overall result in her county in Zambia.

Without you, none of this work would be possible, so thank you for your continued support!

Please visit www.thefathersblessing.org if you want to support or find out more about TFB.

OTHER BOOKS BY IHERINGIUS

Marko Joensuu
*Five Movements: Winning the Battle for Your
Prophetic Gift*
The Red Scorpion: A True Russian Mafia Story
Cloud 913

Claudio Ferro
*Angels and Demons: Modern and Ancient Spiritual
Warfare*

IHERINGIUS

iheringius.com

Lightning Source UK Ltd.
Milton Keynes UK
UKOW02f1318171016

285472UK00001B/3/P